Keeping Softbilled Birds

Colin Vince has been a natural history enthusiast all his life, his special interest in birds beginning when he was given a budgerigar for his ninth birthday. From then on he collected and kept many animals and birds, and at the age of thirteen he started his own aviary. He joined local bird clubs, cycled to zoos on most Saturdays and began exhibiting; some of his birds bred and as his knowledge increased he began to write regularly. His birds won many prizes at exhibitions including his first entry in the junior section of the National Exhibition of Cage and Aviary Birds.

On leaving school, Colin Vince spent almost all his wages on birds and it was about that time that he began to specialize in softbilled species.

The author's attitude to breeding reflects his practical approach to the keeping of softbilled birds. He says, 'You must study their needs and meet every one as perfectly as possible, then if you're lucky some of the birds will breed — but *you* do not breed them.' The success of his methods is shown by the number of his softbills which have bred including grey-winged and Nilgiri blackbirds, shamas, euphonias, white-eyes, summer tanagers and purple-rumped sunbirds.

Colin Vince has been importing birds for many years and in 1973 founded the Tropical Birds Company, making his hobby into his full-time career.

Colin Vince

Keeping Softbilled Birds

Stanley Paul
London Melbourne Sydney Auckland Johannesburg

Stanley Paul & Co. Ltd

An imprint of the Hutchinson Publishing Group

3 Fitzroy Square, London W1P 6JD

Hutchinson Group (Australia) Pty Ltd
30-32 Cremorne Street, Richmond South, Victoria 3121
PO Box 151, Broadway, New South Wales 2007

Hutchinson Group (NZ) Ltd
32-34 View Road, PO Box 40-086, Glenfield, Auckland 10

Hutchinson Group (SA) (Pty) Ltd
PO Box 337, Bergvlei 2012, South Africa

First published 1980
© Colin Vince 1980

Most of the photographs in this book were taken
at the zoological gardens at Walsrode, West Germany,
and we are grateful to this fine establishment for allowing us to reproduce them

Set in VIP Bembo by Input Typesetting Ltd

Printed in Great Britain by The Anchor Press Ltd
and bound by Wm Brendon & Son Ltd,
both of Tiptree, Essex

British Library Cataloguing in Publication Data
   Vince, Colin.
      1. Cage-birds
      I. Title
      636.6'86   SF461

ISBN 0 09 140641 2

Contents

Foreword

Colin Vince's name is synonymous with aviculture.

Readers will be refreshed by his practical and common-sense approach to the subject and by his supreme concern for the welfare of his birds. His critical attitude to present import restrictions is understandable and it is indeed a pity that the pleasures that aviculturists derive from the keeping and scientific study of birds should be jeopardized by those 'dedicated conservationists' who prefer to see the birds exterminated in their respective countries of origin by programmes of forest clearing and urbanization.

Most readers will find the chapter on diets especially interesting and it certainly reminds me that 'variety is the spice of life'.

Although this work is limited to softbills, I am certain that it will have a place on the bookshelves of all aviculturists because the information relating to acclimatization, feeding and general husbandry can be applied to all other bird groups.

Readers will not only enjoy this book, they will also benefit from it.

R. C. J. Sawyer

Introduction

In seeking to define the term 'softbill' one is constantly reminded that there are exceptions to every rule in aviculture. Birds living on fruit, insects or nectar – or perhaps all three – are generally lumped together under this name, but that is a gross oversimplification since all softbills require more than just these in order to maintain good health. If food alone were used to classify birds into their different groups, then logically the lories, lorrikeets and hanging parrots (all parrots which happen to live on fruit and nectar instead of seed) should be called softbills. Wading birds are softbills, yet most people connected with foreign birds would instinctively put them into a separate grouping.

The term 'softbills' implies that the beaks of such birds are physically softer than their seed-eating relatives, the 'hardbills'. When thinking of the fragile beaks of hummingbirds, for example, a case could be made for this theory. Yet what of the woodpeckers? This large family are most definitely softbills though their beaks are hard enough to hammer through trees! The beaks of tiny hardbills such as waxbills are probably softer than those of barbets, crows and other powerfully built softbills.

Little point is served is discussing the whole host of other anomolies which affect a widely used term within avicultural circles, so to maintain the status quo, let us accept, but add to the usual definition of 'softbill' as:

small flying birds which do not live on seed, but some or all of these foods – fruit, insects, nectar, meat and the multi-ingredient insectile mixtures.

1

Why are softbills so popular?

It is not difficult to appreciate the charm of softbills. Generations of aviculturists have been impressed by their colour, their singing ability and their intelligence. It is perhaps their natural friendliness to man that makes many of the familiar softbills so desirable. The lesser-known softbills also invariably develop a good degree of tameness, which rarely occurs with hardbilled birds. Softbills, such as robins and thrushes, together with other species whose natural haunts include gardens, have no real fear of man and so when taken into captivity they quickly settle down and assume strong characters of their own. This tameness is almost impossible to achieve with finches and other regularly kept hardbills. Even after a year, many will still flutter nervously around at the approach of a person, while the average softbill displays little concern for human presence. This tameness, characteristic of so many softbills, helps the aviculturist in two specific ways. Firstly tame birds usually breed more successfully because they do not desert the nest when humans are near; and will accept a wider diet in the form of titbits which benefit the parents and hopefully their young. Secondly, when exhibiting birds, steadiness in the show-cage is vital, so it follows that from two identical exhibits in competition, both of equal quality, if one is tame and the other nervous the former will win.

By selecting from species known to have that natural affinity to man, and by patient training, it is possible to teach softbills simple tricks. As a boy, I had a pet jackdaw which would run after a coin if tossed a few yards, pick it up and fly to the hand. Thereupon he would push it between any two fingers and wait for the process to be repeated! Coming as an injured fledgling at first, it became impossible to get rid of him when he grew up and his injury healed, and so he remained until old age finally caught up with him. At about the same time I purchased an almost naked Indian wagtail from a famous dealer of the period. Only a small price was asked as it was obviously weak and in need of individual treatment which, with a whole roomful of them plus many other birds, the dealer could not reasonably provide. The few feathers were infested with lice but after eradicating them, keeping the bird warm and hand-feeding initially, he gradually improved. My efforts were rewarded eventually by not only a fully feathered Indian wagtail, but a tame one. Though capable of flight, he would follow me around like a minute dog and enjoyed being tucked into the top pocket of my jacket, where he would remain happily for long periods with just his face peering out next to the pens!

Of the several hundred shamas I have handled over the years, most have shown relatively little nervousness once recuperated after arriving from their country of origin. Spiderhunters, too – fairly unusual softbills – come to mind for their surprising tameness.

Taming

Whenever I have wished to tame any softbill, the following procedure has worked well. For the first three weeks in its new environment, the bird is left alone in its cage and, apart from feeding, watering and cleaning, no attempt to tame it is made, since too many simultaneous changes in the life of any bird will induce stress. During this time, it has to accustom itself to its cage, its physical surroundings, the atmosphere of the room, new people and unfamiliar routines. All are entirely different from what it has been used to. When the change in food and water is also considered, it becomes obvious that the total readjustments the bird must make are enormous. On top of all this it has to recover from the inevitable stress of travel. Those first three weeks must therefore be spent as quietly as possible. Any avoidable noise or activity most definitely *should* be avoided, and save for specific medical attention, *no attempt should be made to handle or harass the bird.*

During the next week, the taming process may begin assuming the bird is feeding well and appears lively and healthy. Taking a piece of its favourite food (for most softbills this will probably be a fly or mealworm) offer it from outside the cage. By holding it next to the bars, it will be accessible to the bird who will hesitate initially, but sooner or later snatch it. The best time for this operation is early morning when the main part of the food has been eaten and, from experience, the bird has learned to expect a fresh dish of food. Being hungry and seeing its favourite food held outside the cage, it will eventually give way to temptation. Once the first snatch has been made, the bird will dart back as far as possible to consume the morsel. But it will become bolder and, again spurred by hunger, come back for more. The important points here are not to deliberately deprive the bird of food in the hope of achieving this step faster, for a starving bird is more likely to die than submit to taming. Furthermore, all birds have different temperaments and each will vary in the time taken to snatch offerings. The entire process must be one of patiently gaining the bird's confidence.

When several morsels are taken and its appetite satisfied, the routine should be followed at least once daily, but preferably more often, for another week. Then instead of offering the food from outside the cage, do it with the hand *inside*. The bird will hesitate at first but when this has been successfully carried out, continue the daily routine for at least a week more. Finally, with the hand inside the cage, hold the food just out of reach – forcing the bird to hop on to the hand to get it. When this action becomes routine to the bird, the cage door is opened and food held prominently just outside it. The bird should by now have achieved a high degree of tameness and while first standing on the doorstep to reach the offerings, should soon hop on to the hand *outside* its cage for food. It then becomes just a matter of time for complete tameness to follow, whereby the bird will willingly leave its cage when the door is opened and fly to its owner in search of food and eventually become quite humanized.

Low cost of keeping

With careful housekeeping it is possible to maintain softbills for little more expense than hardbills. This is brought about by the tremendous increase in seed prices over recent years. By making friends with local greengrocers and bakers, I have always found it possible to buy damaged fruit and stale cakes very cheaply. Similarly, butchers will sometimes sell their small offcuts of beef, chicken and other meat at reasonable prices. When minced, these items form another important basic softbill food. Friendly neighbourhood butchers are not so numerous, however, as their counterparts in greengrocery and bakery – probably because all meat offcuts can profitably be made into sausages. Apart from beef and chicken, other meat is not so desirable for softbill feeding as it is often very fatty and its chemistry does not always agree with the digestion of anything but *Corvidae* species (crows).

Colourful plumage

The most obvious attraction of softbills is colour. Of course there are certain species unable to boast attractive plumage but these are few. With softbills the rule is colour – in some spectacularly so. Evolution has provided many with remarkable adornments, usually for court-ship or as aids to specialized feeding, as well as simply colourful plumage. The head plumes, ruffs, hoods and fantastic tails of many birds of paradise are supreme in the bird kingdom. The iridescent beauty of most hummingbirds and their incredible beak structures – the swordbill with a bill longer than its whole body, the sicklebill whose name so accurately describes the shape of its beak, the thornbill whose short, thin beak is again accurately reflected in its common name. Then there are the hummingbirds with fantastic tails, like the train bearers, streamer tails and sylphs; those with frills and hoods such as the minute coquettes. The fabulous cotingas from Ecuador, Colombia and Brazil – rarely seen in captivity as they are difficult to catch from the heights of the forest canopy they inhabit – are among the most brilliantly coloured softbills imaginable. Fairy bluebirds, tanagers, honeycreepers, pittas, sunbirds are among the more fre-quently available species and are just a few examples of the extreme beauty of softbills.

Song

In the world of hardbills, there are few noted songsters, yet vocal accomplishments are commonplace among softbills. Some such as the shama, are famous for the beauty of their song and that, allied to its tameness, is a major reason for its traditional following in many Asiatic countries. For centuries the Chinese have made pets of shamas, zosterops, fruitsuckers, magpie robins, mesias, and various thrushes; housing them in ornamental cages so that their song could be enjoyed. Some of the old cages, especially the tiny ones for zosterops, are true works of art – very often made in the form of pagodas, complete with balconies, ornamental doors and all delicately painted with minute traditional patterns. Tiny hand-painted feeding cups, made from wafer-thin china, are hooked inside special little side doors and the whole creation obviously made with great craftsmanship.

In these more enlightened times we do not approve of keeping birds in small cages, and with the impetus of bird conservation, most aviculturists are quite rightly providing well-furnished aviaries, in which every effort is made to breed softbills as well as other birds. With man continually destroying natural habitat, forcing many soft-bills into a vulnerable position, all captive breeding attempts are important.

Though the methods of keeping them have changed, the fact still remains that softbills are popular throughout the world for the beauty of their song as much as anything else. The shama – arguably the best softbill songster – is capable of the most marvellous singing imaginable.

Cleaning cages

Providing they are of sufficient size for what they house, many softbills may reasonably be caged. Singletons which cannot be paired, or aggressive cock softbills are normally housed in this way. Indeed caging has many advantages which will be discussed in the chapter on housing. It has always been a major advantage of caged softbills, as opposed to caged hardbills, that they are not untidy. They do not generate seed husks which, when the birds fly, get absolutely everywhere. Sand and grit similarly does not spread around the room since softbills do not require these items. The cage floor is best covered with a few sheets of clean newspaper, and when soiled, simply rolled up and destroyed. For ease of servicing, all cages should have a tray covering the actual floor, and it is upon this that the paper is spread. Only seconds are needed to remove the tray and renew the paper, which contrasts favourably with the scraping and sweeping so necessary with hardbills. This point is sometimes belaboured by softbill devotees but it is certainly a big advantage when balancing softbill maintenance against that of hardbills.

Cleaning aviaries

Maintaining softbills in aviaries will also be covered under housing but, whilst looking at what makes softbills so popular, it must be mentioned that when kept in a natural planted aviary, cleaning out as such is almost non-existent. If not overcrowded, the aviary will remain wholesome for long periods as the watery droppings of most softbills quickly become absorbed in the earth, enriching its fertility and assisting plant growth. It is only under roosting perches that mounds of droppings occur, and these must of course be removed, perhaps twice weekly. Old food particles must also be cleared, and the bare ground areas raked to keep a neat appearance. The majority of softbill aviaries are easier to keep tidy than those occupied by hardbills, because of the different nature of their droppings. Plant life, assisted by the moist softbill droppings, is largely impossible in hardbill aviaries as hardbills destroy foliage. Also the typical white droppings of hardbills *must*, on both hygienic and aesthetic grounds, be washed away regularly.

Feeding

Softbill diets are certainly more complex than those for hardbills, but not tremendously so. In any case it is wrong to compare their various needs with 'just the handful of seed' one sometimes hears being claimed as the standard hardbill diet. My hardbills have various seeds, greenfood, fruit, insects, bread soaked in milk, and other things. A wide diet is necessary for *any* bird to achieve perfect health, so in that sense a softbill diet is not as complicated as some hardbill enthusiasts believe. Detailed discussion on feeding softbills is in the chapter on feeding.

Varieties of species

When thinking of the world bird population, it soon becomes apparent that there are more softbill species than any others. Even allowing for the enormous number which, for one reason or another, are never seen in captivity, there is still plenty for the softbill aviculturist to choose from. Due, however, to their wide and diverse families, some softbills are easier to maintain in captivity than others. Indeed, if a scale of bird's suitability for captivity were drawn up, with any number of grades, there would be a softbill for every one. At one end are the mynahs, so robust they will thrive in very inexperienced hands, and at the other such subjects as swifts which are not suited to captivity at all. In between are hundreds of species which with varying degrees of success, have been maintained in captivity.

Broadly speaking, softbills are classified into five groups:

Omnivores are perhaps the easiest as they eat a wide variety of foods and will generally adapt well to changed circumstances. This group contains most of the recommended beginner's species.

Frugivores, the next most adaptable, are blessed with gross appetites and are simple to feed. If a bird eats well, the chances are it won't fall ill. As the name suggests, fruit is the largest item on their menu, but by no means the *only* one.

Nectivores include many undemanding species, but others are only suitable for experienced aviculturists. Nectar forms the major food but again, many other things are required to provide a balanced diet.

Insectivores without doubt constitute the biggest challenge as most will look at nothing but live insects at first, and it is no easy task to transfer them to a captive (or substitute) diet. In addition, many insectivores 'hawk' flying insects naturally, and these are the most difficult of all.

Carnivores include such exciting softbills as kingfishers and Abyssinian ground hornbills. Many are big birds usually kept by zoos, but any softbill enthusiast with suitable accommodation should find them quite simple to maintain in good health.

The last part of the book describes a selection from each group.

2

How we get them

Outside pressures affecting aviculture

For many years a combination of outside pressures have 'controlled' the activities of all those involved with birds. Literally every link in the chain has been affected, from original trapper (many of whom have been forced out of business) to exporter, to importer, to final purchasing aviculturist. Whilst many aspects of the international bird trade would have benefited from informed and sensible control, vast bureaucratic wheels have all but rolled the life blood out of it. Because many exporting countries have yielded to the demands of international conservation pressure groups, and banned the export of their birds, less variety is available to the foreign aviculturist. Other countries, like India, have banned the export of specific species, though not uncommon species which could perhaps be considered vulnerable, such as the super-abundant finches and mynahs. Colombia and Paraguay, two traditional South American exporting countries, recently fell into line by banning the export of everything. The powerful groups, able to influence governments to that extent, no doubt claim each ban as a victory – deluding themselves that each bird not exported for aviculture will live to a contented old age in its natural environment.

Yet this form of conservation is not working. Destruction of habitat still goes on at an enormous pace, and that – not the reasonable needs of international aviculture – is the biggest killer of birds. The relentless process of 'deforestation' saws, drags and bulldozes literally millions of trees off the face of the world's jungles every week. In rapidly developing Brazil alone, figures of several thousand acres being deforested weekly are often quoted.

Though only concerned with its effects on bird life in this book, destruction of the world's forests on this scale involves wider issues than a nation's desire to sell its timber and build modern roads and cities. Bare forest earth can degenerate into desert; rain forests of the tropics generate water, so with deforestation *that* becomes scarcer and the balance of the very atmosphere itself, scientists tell us, can become adversely affected.

Many softbilled birds, and other forest creatures, are territorial. Each will find, barring a natural catastrophe, enough food in its own territory and defend it against intruders. This pattern only changes at breeding times. If a percentage of forest is obliterated in the name of progress, what happens to its wild life? It naturally penetrates the remaining forest but, in the case of many softbill species, that will involve the invasion of another's territory. A fight results, the new-comers being chased on to another established territory. The process may be repeated several times until, being weakened by each encounter and insufficient food, the displaced birds often die. Should they be lucky enough to enter territory held by an old or injured bird, they may win the fight and survive themselves but in most cases not. Flock birds which travel freely through the various territories are not harassed so much, but if enough forest is removed their food supply becomes jeopardized since what remains could not support a greatly increased population.

Every year in poor tropical countries, millions of softbills are killed and eaten as a delicacy. There is no excuse for this in those Mediterranean countries which have a reasonable or good standard of living. This regular slaughter features in the press, yet what do the various conservation pressure groups do about it? It seems that all their efforts are spent further 'controlling' the art of aviculture. Almost all birds come into aviculture from what are commonly termed 'third world' or 'developing' countries. Most of their populations are desperately poor, so if *they* kill softbills or anything else for food, we blessed with full bellies should not criticize them. Yet prior to the harassment of aviculture, some of these people were better off. They were the bird trappers, many specializing in softbills, and with the money earned could enjoy at least something approaching a proper diet. Now they are forced to eat the birds. These poor people suffer, aviculture suffers, the birds suffer; and the conservationists are satisfied.

Australia is not a poor or backward or poverty-stricken country, but here a different paradox exists. Certain of her birds are both abundant and destructive to crops. From time to time an open season is created, enabling anybody with a gun to kill them, not for food, but for sport. The same government which encourages this killing will not allow a single bird to be sent overseas, where foreign aviculturists would welcome what is to them a special bird and lavish every care on it. There are ways, however, by claiming that they are non-profit-making organizations, that certain zoos have imported Australian birds occasionally.

Once established, softbills along with other birds usually live far longer in captivity than in the wild, since in captivity they receive regular food and water and have no predators. Critics say that captivity deprives birds of flying space and, no matter how big the aviary, this is essentially true. Nevertheless with massive destruction of natural habitat, with killing for food, with shooting for sport and endless harassment by man, it does seem illogical that aviculture should be so hounded.

Instead of banning everything and yet continuing destruction of habitat, would it not be better to organize a sensible and *simple* trapping procedure for aviculture? Trapping just prior to deforestation programmes could be done under experienced local supervision, and the birds only handled by people with a good proven record of bird husbandry and in possession of suitable accommodation. Many professional bird exporters fall into this category, and if the receiving aviculturists were of similar specification, the birds would stand a far better chance of survival, and hopefully eventual captive breeding, than if left to face the bulldozer and gun.

Some softbills are endangered now. How sad it will be (and who will know?) if individuals of some precarious species lose out against man and his machines.

Trapping softbills

Most trapping techniques have their origins in the last century, and vary from country to country. There are all sorts of trap cages, some manually operated by pulling a long cord attached to the door, so that it snaps shut as soon as the hidden trapper sees a suitable bird enter. Others with spring-loaded doors are automatic and usually rely on the weight of the bird landing on a food dish just inside the cage to set it off.

The Indians are past masters at bird liming. By this method several small softbills may be caught at once if the trapper has studied their routine in advance. Once it is known that a party of perhaps yuhinas or some similar small babblers, regularly visit a certain tree, the most likely twigs are coated with bird lime, a type of resin. Alighting on the sticky twigs, the birds will remain fast until removed by the trapper. He will then wash their feet free of the glue and place them in a cotton bag to transport home or, if he does not possess holding cages, direct to an exporter. The exporter will buy from the trapper and assemble orders for his overseas customers.

Larger softbills in India, especially those who spend much time on the ground, such as pittas and thrushes, are also caught with lime, but their capture is individual and requires a very special skill. A well-lined cotton ball is fixed to one end of a long whippy bamboo. Whilst skulking in the undergrowth, the trapper will spot a bird and very slowly edge the pole towards it. When the glued ball is as near as possible to the bird, a wrist action flips the pole, sticking the bird to it. Skill also dictates how to roll the catch while pulling the pole back. Too much causes the plumage to be badly glued, necessitating a moult before the bird looks perfect again. Too little and he will be away – leaving just a patch of feathers stuck to the glue ball!

In a lot of South-East Asian countries and some in South America, baby softbills are taken from the nest and hand reared. Numerous species have been hand reared by native trappers, though in practice the method is reserved more for deep hole nesters like bee-eaters, toucans and hornbills. The trapper must know his stuff here, too, for ideally he has to dig into the nest and remove the chicks when they are near to fledging. If taken very young, the hand rearing is a longer and much more tedious job. The South American Amerindians have traditionally kept pet birds in their jungle villages, invariably hand rearing chicks taken from the nest. Such birds, because of their human contact, are always very tame and from the avicultural viewpoint far superior to wild-caught ones.

Traditional trapping methods such as these have been largely obscured by the more recently invented mist-net, which is now used extensively in trapping areas. Its limitations are that it can only cope with birds occupying a band about 1 to 6 metres from the ground. It was probably developed in Japan, and it is there that the finest ones are still made. In essence a giant ladies' hairnet with horizontal strings forming pockets, it is erected between poles and, as flying birds cannot see it, they collide with it, falling into the pocket immediately underneath them. They must then be removed by the trapper – like most things in his trade, this requires a lot of practice to achieve perfection – and placed in a bag for transport home. With mist-nets, there is virtually no chance of birds harming themselves, and when not in use the nets compress into a tiny parcel of no significant weight.

Transportation

I can think of only three countries where the trapper is also the exporter. In all other cases, it is the exporter who buys from the actual trapper and despatches to overseas destinations. The exporter is an educated man, unlike most trappers, and has various bird accom-

modation, often with staff to help look after the birds. He will probably be able to compose a letter in English and will be familiar with
airline procedures, together with local regulations relative to his business. It is while in the exporter's hands that newly caught softbills
receive a form of establishment, but since his foods and animal husbandry are probably not as good as ours, this process must begin
afresh upon importation.

Aviculturists of past generations had only sea transportation by
which birds could be carried. Softbill aviculture was probably at its
best at the beginning of this century, when wealthy estate owners,
frequently titled, vied with each other in developing the most com-
prehensive collections. They organized and paid for major expeditions
to all corners of the tropics; and on almost every occasion some
previously unknown softbill species were brought back to grace their
remarkable aviaries. Those undertaking such trips had to know
exactly what they were doing, for apart from actually catching the
birds, they had to bring them back by long and often perilous sea
journeys. It is a credit to the skill of these gentlemen that after
sometimes months of sea travel, the delicate birds arrived alive and
well. Even with the vastly superior knowledge of softbill's dietary
needs which we now have, it is doubtful whether anybody today
could emulate their achievements.

Exporters now send all birds, in especially designed boxes, by air
to the overseas importer. Theoretically birds should be given special
treatment and some priority en route, but being unaccompanied they
are often treated improperly and as a result they – and softbills especially – arrive in poor condition quite often. Even when they do arrive
at the importer's airport, several hours elapse before the importer can
actually take them away. Birds travel in the cargo holds of planes
and, in order that they may feed en route, the holds should be lit.
When flying in non-tropical areas, the holds should also be heated. It
has never been possible to get clear information on these points, and
the indications are that in most cases holds are neither lit nor heated.
It is not unusual for other cargo to be tightly packed around livestock,
thus endangering its air supply. A lorry meets planes on landing and
all cargo is then loaded and driven to the warehouse. This operation
is usually long so the birds suffer greatly from prolonged exposure to
dangerously low temperatures, the noise of cargo clattering all around
them and the general turmoil of the tarmac.

So much stress and suffering could be avoided if a small van were
used exclusively for livestock at this point in the transport procedure.
It need cost nothing as airlines have many such vehicles. Once in the
warehouse, airline staff prepare certain documents, send them to the

customs officer and wait for him to clear the birds. It is at this stage that the worst delays of all occur. At London airport birds are delayed anything up to four hours awaiting clearance – exceptionally longer. During this time weak birds which could probably be saved, often die. This is especially true of small softbills but applies to all birds. Airline staff are generally uninterested, explaining that they have done their part and all concerned must now wait for the customs officer to clear the consignment. The customs officer is regarded with great subservience and when, after some hours waiting, the frustrated importer may demand to see him personally, airline staff will try hard to dissuade him. It was recently pointed out to me when in this very situation that to press the customs officer could result in him taking even longer! The airline had earlier said some of the birds were dead and others looking weak so, with the overwhelming desire to get them into quarantine and administer to their needs, I *did* press and as far as I could tell, my efforts *did* result in greater delays!

The simple process of customs clearance could, with goodwill, common sense and co-operation, be carried out in minutes. That would virtually eliminate deaths at the airport and those occurring soon after caused by airport delays.

The importer will utter a heartfelt 'Hallelujah' or something of the sort when he hears the magic words 'They're cleared now'. Money changes hands, simple form-filling completed – and he staggers incredulous to join the queue at the warehouse door. Among lorries loading giant crates and irate travellers wanting their cases, he will wait . . . and wait. In the fullness of time, a warehouseman brings the birds on a fork-lift truck. Now, after God knows how many hours and so much worry that he is thinner than when he went in, the importer may take his surviving birds into quarantine.

The point is so fundamental, and so easy to achieve that I make no apologies for repeating it: whilst some mortality in air transportation of birds, particularly softbills, is inevitable, it is far higher than it need be, for reasons quite beyond the control of exporter or importer.

Enormous numbers of birds would live which now die if:

a)   the airlines lit the cargo holds when carrying livestock;
b)   they heated the holds when flying in non-tropical areas;
c)   they did not place other cargo around livestock cages to the extent that their air supply was endangered;
d)   at destination airport, the birds were offloaded on to one of the small airline vans and quickly taken to the warehouse, keeping separate from other cargo, and
e)   customs officers would exercise a little co-operation, actually

talking to the importer in the event of queries, and genuinely give top priority to livestock.

Quarantine

Quarantine regulations apply to imported birds in most countries nowadays and British ones are typical. On being released to him at the airport, the importer must immediately deliver the birds to a proper quarantine building. Earlier inspection and approval will have been given by the Ministry of Agriculture, for both vehicle and building; and this organization oversees the birds while serving their statutory five weeks in quarantine. The quarantining of softbills calls for much attention to detail since most have to be treated as individuals – weaklings, those in the moult and those requiring highly specialized diets all need personal attention. Veterinary inspectors check the birds weekly and only they, Ministry inspectors and the regular attendant may enter the building.

Acclimatization and establishment

During quarantine the vital processes of acclimatizing and establishing are carried out to a large extent. People are generally aware of the need to acclimatize tropical birds but few consider the even more important process of establishing. This basically means training the birds to accept a new diet, new environment, new people of unfamiliar colour and behaviour, new atmosphere and captive conditions with their inevitable flight restrictions. Establishing obviously accompanies acclimatizing – the two being inter-related - but one without the other is of little value.

Depending on their natural environment, I normally maintain a temperature of 25 to 30°C for the first week and dull night lights are left on, to maximize the opportunities for feeding. During travel, the hours of darkness when feeding was not possible, plus the associated stress of the journey, have to be counteracted in this way. Tanagers and other sociable softbills (except weaklings) may be housed collectively, but all insectivores and known aggressors are caged individually. To avoid panic, and enable a form of trust to develop, work has to be done quietly and everything possible done to avoid noise. Cleaning out necessitates much movement so this is deliberately put off for the first three days. Medication is given under veterinary supervision where necessary, though the blanket administration of a standard antibiotic is helpful with softbills. The stress of the journey, and loss of body heat resulting from insufficient food intake and inadequacies of the transport system, often cause a fatal imbalance of intestinal bacteria. Certain bacteria live naturally in the intestines and are harmless in a fit bird. In a weak one, however, the more virile bacteria multiply rapidly, unbalancing the bird's body chemistry and likely to cause death. Specified antibiotics check this bacterial 'flare up' and, if administered under veterinary direction, with the back-up laboratory investigation of samples, great benefits are possible.

The food of all softbills in quarantine, particularly for the first critical week, is laced with mineral, protein and vitamin preparations since every effort must be made to get the birds back into condition. Most will be lighter than they should be – the breast bone feeling quite prominent – proving that very little had been consumed during the journey. Everything possible is therefore done in quarantine to rectify this situation and produce a plump, healthy bird at the end of the period.

Tremendous patience and some simple tricks are necessary in getting most insectivores on to a diet that is not 100 per cent living insects. Again for the first all-important week, there is little attempt to do this since the immediate requirement is that the birds should eat. It matters not at that stage exactly what they do eat – the objective initially is just that they replace lost weight. During the following four weeks of quarantine, they will learn (albeit unwillingly) to accept modest amounts of inanimate foods.

Apart from insectivores, softbills from the other groups are less difficult in establishing, and whilst in quarantine they too will gradually be weaned from the foods they were used to overseas on to the normal avicultural diets.

All my softbills will also have experienced a gradual reduction in temperature from the original 25 to 30°C, to 16 to 18°C. So the establishing process is largely done during quarantine, and also the worst part of acclimatizing. Whether the birds are now hardy enough to be transferred to an outdoor aviary depends entirely on the time of year. In this important respect, acclimatization must now be further expanded.

Completing the acclimatization process

Although a bird may have been established to captivity and acclimatized during quarantine, from tropical temperatures to about 16°C, it would be ridiculous to transfer it to an outdoor aviary if the outside temperature is freezing! It is surprising, however, that some people expect such a transfer to work.

Softbills are fairly easy to completely acclimatize, but the entire process takes up to a year and can only begin during the summer because that is when the weather is warmest and daylight hours longest. During June, for example, a softbill could be taken from quarantine and released into an outdoor aviary with every chance of success. The same bird released in October would probably die. By transferring in the summer, temperatures both indoors and outdoors are approximately the same, so the movement can comfortably be tolerated. Although aviaries will be discussed under housing, it is important to mention here that softbill aviaries must be well protected from bad weather. A house part, which always contains the food, is best as new birds may be released into that at first and not let out. After a day or two they may be given the freedom of the whole aviary – house and flight during daytime – but ideally chased into the house part and shut in at night. Following a week of this procedure, most will roost in the house as routine and remain safe from heavy rain and night frights as a result.

As the year progresses, the birds become used to gradual temperature reductions and take them in their stride. Unexpected drops in temperature and the less common warm spells are all experienced – but without harm since until winter itself comes, the temperatures are all within a tolerable band. Additionally, showers are experienced with all other climatic variations so typical of this part of the world. The birds become truly 'weathered' and at the approach of winter have to be sorted according to their hardiness. Here is a selection of softbills which can stay in the aviary for the whole winter, subject only to minor diet adjustments and being chased into their house at nights: starlings, jays, magpies, thrushes, pekin robins, bulbuls, mountain tanagers and other largish tanagers, hornbills, the larger babblers, touracos, toucans, mesias, sibias, shrikes, laughing thrushes, drongos, kiskadees. These and many others will survive the winter and so become 100 per cent acclimatized.

The less hardy softbills have at this point reached the safe limit in acclimatization and should be housed indoors for the winter itself. If the house part of the aviary is large enough and has a heater and light, they could be confined to this for the winter, whilst being let out for the odd unseasonal warm day. If the house part is not suitable or of sufficient size, the birds must be housed in roomy cages indoors for the winter. Typical subjects in this group are hummingbirds, sunbirds, spiderhunters, honeycreepers, all tanagers smaller than the mountain, yuhinas, pittas, barbets, woodpeckers, flycatchers, tits, chats, fruit pigeons, broadbills, flowerpeckers, ioras, redstarts, all small species of babblers. In the absence of expert advice, a rough guide as to which species may be left out and which are only half hardy is body size. Generally speaking the larger ones are the hardier. Also take the feet into consideration. Terrestrial species such as pittas will be in danger of frostbite even if they can withstand coldness. Softbills from high altitudes are obviously more suited to all-round outdoor existence than those from hot plains.

The omnivores include most of those capable of wintering out. They are easy to cater for – which helps when it is realized that the diets of birds staying outdoors will have to be slightly amended for winter. The reduction of body temperature is serious, as explained earlier, and this can happen rapidly when birds are sleeping during very cold nights. Although a slight heat loss is normal during sleep, severe coldness can reduce body heat to dangerous levels, so extra carbohydrates must be added to the winter diets. Cheese and beef fat (suet) are excellent items for inclusion in winter diets, and it is recommended that sunflower oil (available from health food shops) be added to the insectile mixture. Finally, an extra helping of mealworms should adequately counteract the loss of body heat problems. Return to the normal diets however in spring, or over-fat birds will be the result! Diets of the half-hardy softbills overwintered in temperatures not below 6 to 8°C, do not need adjustment, though extra mealworms will be of value. For nectivores being overwintered, it helps a lot to squeeze a few mealworms into their nectar. Depending on local weather conditions, the half-hardy species are usually safe to be returned to the aviary in late March, if they have been overwintered indoors. It will be between then and September that the first captive breeding may take place. Breeding activities during this time may also be expected of the less demanding omnivores which have wintered outdoors.

Although the half-hardy ones will have to be overwintered in the same fashion every year, complete acclimatization is said to have taken place when they have successfully been reintroduced to the aviary around March, and remained there until autumn. In other words, one year on from when the procedure first started. During that time they will have experienced all weather conditions *within their band of tolerance*. The larger, tougher species which have wintered outdoors without artificial warmth will similarly have experienced all conditions, though more extreme, and they too, after the year, will be completely acclimatized.

I recap since the distinction is important: proper acclimatization can only begin in the warm months and is a one-year process. Strong species will have spent a full twelve months literally outdoors. Less hardy ones require heat during the winter but even so, when the year has passed, they are as acclimatized as it is possible for them to be.

3

Purchasing

In these days of quarantine it is virtually impossible for an unwell softbill to be offered for sale, so much standard advice to purchasers no longer applies. The supervising veterinary officers will have attended to any illness during quarantine and checked, on the final inspection, that all the birds are well. Nevertheless there are certain criteria which can be used when selecting softbills, and these are as valid today as they ever were.

Probably the most important thing to check is the vent since residues of tainted droppings, compacted droppings stuck to vent feathers, swellings of the vent and obvious odours are all to be regarded with suspicion. In short the vent should be clean and dry, with surrounding feathers in the same condition. Eyes should be bright and quite glossy. Many softbills have large eyes which show any imperfections more clearly. For a variety of reasons, the eyes of softbills sometimes attract bacteria which causes them to water and frequently close. Conjunctivitis is usually to blame but fortunately, if treated early, is easy to cure. Nostrils are important – they should be unblocked and dry, showing no discharge.

The general plumage is of no real concern since damaged, missing or soiled feathers will always moult out and be replaced with perfect new ones. It is surprising how many aviculturists are more impressed by plumage condition then anything else – yet one of aviculture's chief pleasures is seeing a scruffy bird moult out into a feathered gem! It is sometimes necessary to buy a softbill in the moult, and although ideally they should remain where they are until it is completed, this is seldom possible. There is no great danger in moving moulting birds providing the journey is quick and quiet. Their new environment should be as close as possible to what they have been used to, at least until the moult is completed. One must be sensitive to the needs of a moulting softbill, which will be in lower condition and more prone to stress than usual.

Other considerations in purchasing softbills depend on whether they are required for exhibiting. If they are, attention must be paid to the feet since missing claws, imperfectly formed or damaged claws, lumps on the feet, all attract reduced points from exhibition judges.

If ever there was a case for altering the judging system, this is surely it. Foot imperfections are common in softbills – all occur in the country of origin, often while the bird is still a nestling – so it seems illogical to penalize the owner for something quite outside his control. Hundreds of magnificent softbills must exist which could excel at exhibitions if it were not perhaps for one slightly twisted claw. See that there are no beak imperfections and that wings are of equal length, not crossed at the tips or hung unevenly.

If not required for exhibition primarily or exclusively, then such faults are totally unimportant. Softbills being purchased for breeding may possess several of these exhibition faults without their breeding potential being impaired one iota. Indeed life is so perverse that I have known successful breedings take place among pairs which, between them, possessed just about every exhibition fault in the book, while perfect pairs have done nothing! Successful breeding pairs sometimes comprise non-flyers, one legged hens, cocks with severe foot imperfections and either sex where blindness has occurred in one eye.

Purchasing softbills without the later intention to exhibit them is a less critical operation, and if breeding is hoped for it is more important to select plump, lively birds of inquisitive natures and which look likely to tame easily.

It is not always possible to visit the seller if long distances and modest purchases are involved, but personal selection is strongly recommended when purchasing softbills just as much as any other birds. The reasons are obvious, really – you are your own judge and unlikely to buy birds you do not like the look of. By noting the conditions and diet, it is easier to match what the birds have been used to when you get home. As stressed earlier, if the conditions pertaining during quarantine can be fairly closely followed *initially* when moving to a new environment, the birds should have no problems readjusting. Changes the purchaser may wish to make – to bring new birds into his own routine – should be done *gradually*.

Some aviculturists are terrified at the thought of having birds sent by train. There is certainly a risk involved but fortunately mishaps are fairly rare. Though as a percentage of the whole those rail despatches which do go wrong are very small, the situation is far from satisfactory. Against a background of big and regular price increases, British Rail's conditions of carriage effectively relieve them of responsibility for anything. Whenever birds arrive excessively late, sometimes having perished during their ordeal, the official response to complaints is to express regret but point to the conditions of carriage. It is usually possible to show some form of negligence if a bird takes two days to arrive at a destination normally possible in, say sixteen hours, but even so, not a penny compensation is paid.

It is obvious that every effort should be made to personally collect delicate species such as nectivores and insectivores, though I regularly despatch them and in most instances they reach their destinations safely. The risk is small enough to accept, however, when dealing with the more robust frugivores and omnivores. Even allowing for *modest* delays during train journeys, most of these birds are strong enough when acclimatized to withstand them. I emphasize however that *all* birds should be personally collected if at all possible. It is an interesting point that the purchaser could collect his birds and still reach his home by *train* in less than half the time it would take for the birds, travelling as unaccompanied packages, to arrive. When having birds despatched by train, it is the responsibility of the sender to prepare a suitable box. This will differ according to what it is to contain – a box for a treepie, for example, will have to be stronger and with different furnishings than that for a sunbird. From the purchaser's point of view, the vital thing is to get complete dietary and management details from the supplier well in advance; then have everything ready for receiving the new birds. The cage must be prepared, with suitable food and a dish of slightly warmed water *before* the birds arrive, so that upon receipt they can go in immediately. Leave well alone for the rest of the day and keep in mind the earlier mentioned points about minimizing stress and overcoming the effects of the journey.

4

Housing

Reception cages

Whether collected personally or received by train, newly purchased softbills should be caged individually in a bright room heated to a temperature of about 16°C if the weather is cold. The cage need not be as big as permanent cages (flight cages) discussed next, and the initial temperature can be reduced after the first week by a degree a day. Those few extra degrees at first are helpful in overcoming the effects of the train journey but are not necessary for longer than a week. Detailed checks on food consumption, indicating possible dietary adjustments, are easy while being housed in this way. Furthermore each bird can sleep as long as it wishes without interruptions from companions, eat the choicest foods without competition, and generally recuperate in peace.

Reception cages are not used after one to two weeks. The birds are then transferred to *permanent accommodation* which may be any of the following:

Flight cages in a birdroom

This is the traditional form of housing softbills favoured particularly by exhibitors. It is basically a longish cage made from wood or metal sheeting all over, except for the barred or wire meshed front. With singletons of species which will not tolerate each other (and many softbill favourites are solitary by nature) or where outdoor accommodation is unavailable, a room containing several such cages enables a variety of softbills to be adequately maintained. Rooms of this type may be a suitably insulated garden shed, or a spare room of the house. They are referred to as 'birdrooms' and, apart from cages, some have small aviaries built in them, together with storage cupboards, sinks and all sorts of comforts. It is not unusual for dedicated aviculturists to have a carpet and armchair in the middle of their birdrooms!

The smallest possible flight cage should be 90 cm long by 30 cm deep by 35 cm high, (see Fig. 1) and this would accommodate a pair of small softbills like zosterops, or one single specimen the size of a bulbul. If caged, sunbirds and hummingbirds must be kept singly since they are aggressive with their own kind in confined areas and will fight. Flight cages are *not* as perfect as aviary accommodation, and of course provide no breeding possibilities whatsoever, but it is not cruel to house most softbills in them providing they are as large as possible and certainly not less than indicated above. They also have the enormous advantage listed under Reception cages which cannot be provided within aviaries.

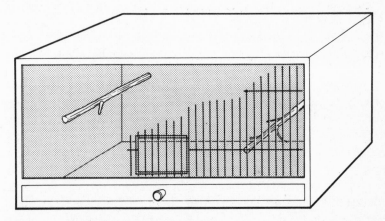

Figure 1 *Flight cage suitable for softbills*

Flight cages in birdrooms are invariably painted with white interiors and black exteriors, but this colour scheme is stark and any colours may be used except the luminous hues. Pastel interiors with brighter outsides are attractive. Apart from woodpeckers and, to a lesser degree, barbets, softbills do not peck their cages so the lead content of paint – so worrying for parrot aviculturists – is immaterial.

For small softbills, a twiggy branch fixed near each end of the cage provides adequate perching, though the larger species require one fixed perch at each end, of between 1 cm, and 2 cm diameter. If the cage is long enough, a couple of extra perches may be placed at varying heights about midway between the two end ones. In each instance, natural twigs and branches of *varying* diameters are recommended. They are better for the feet and should be replaced when they either dry out or become badly soiled – whichever happens first. Most softbills have fairly soft feet which are inclined to develop sores if regular-diameter hardwood dowels are used as perching. Also the varying diameters and surfaces of natural twigs exercise the feet which, in rare and extreme instances, have become virtually set in one position by having only one-diameter hardwood dowels. Although the exact position of perches is not critical, softbills with long tails need sufficient clearance from both floor and walls.

Floor covering for flight cages is best restricted to several layers of newspaper, which is absorbent and easy to replace. Nectivores require more frequent cleaning out as their droppings are largely liquid. For those and most frugivores, newspaper should be changed every two days. Other softbills have more solid droppings by nature of their diets, and so a cleaning programme involving new paper twice-weekly is all right for them. Sawdust has some advantages as floor covering, but the fluttering of the birds blows it to the edges of the tray, leaving the centre largely bare. Sand must not be used for softbill cages as it irritates their delicate feet.

Food containers in flight cages present few problems. Special nectar tubes are available for hummingbirds and these may be hung either inside or outside the cage. It is most practical to hang them outside with just the red drinking spout through the bars. A saucer of slightly warm water for bathing is then placed centrally on the cage floor. For all other softbills including other nectivores I have always used shallow dishes, for both food and water. Plastic dishes approximately 10 to 12 cm diameter and 3 cm deep are generally satisfactory, but thick china ones are sometimes necessary for heavy softbills, the weight of which overturns plastic dishes when they stand on their edges. Rollers, motmots and mynahs are typical examples of such softbills.

Outdoor aviaries

Normal aviary designs are basically acceptable for all softbills but whatever types are to be so housed, greater protection from adverse weather is required than would be necessary for birds such as budgerigars and canaries. A great deal of discomfort is avoidable if heavy gauge polythene is fixed over most of the wire netted areas during winter. If simple frames are made, with the polythene stretched over them, it is possible to screw them into position for winter, and remove for the summer. Sections of a metre square usually withstand winds, but bigger areas will rip. Clear corrugated PVC sheeting is ideal for roof covering and all the roof of the house part, plus good areas of the flight roof, should be covered with this material. If the *whole* of the flight roof is covered, the advantages of greater protection can be outweighed by rain not reaching the shrubs, which will die unless regularly watered by hand.

Figure 2 illustrates a conventional outdoor aviary, comprising a covered house part plus open wire-netted flight. For seed-eating birds the flight is normally quite spartan since they destroy any plant growth. However the majority of softbills are not destructive to any appreciable extent, so planted aviaries are the norm. This is all to the good as natural nesting sites are created and the whole aviary is far more attractive.

If building an outdoor aviary, there are certain fundamental points not to be overlooked, irrespective of the size or shape of it, which are governed by the availability of ground and money. As with all buildings, bad design features are costly and inconvenient to rectify so it is well worth considering everything very fully at design stage, before buying any materials. The house part is invariably glossed over in aviary designs, with disproportionate attention being paid to the much larger outside flight. This is understandable as the flight gives scope for artistic landscaping and is the part mostly occupied by the birds – however tropical softbills and our winters do not go together. It is at these times when the inadequacies of the typical house part become so apparent: small areas, poorly lit and ventilated, entry holes without doors and so on. *At least equal* thought must be given to the house part as the flight when planning a softbill aviary, remembering that the birds should be physically shut in for winter nights, and will therefore spend more time during those months inside than out. The merits of doing this are considerable yet I have never seen such advice published. As mentioned in the chaper on acclimatization, softbill diets must be enriched during winter to counteract lower temperatures and reduced daylight hours (feeding hours) associated with winter. Even so, protection from severe winter nights reduces the risks of losses enormously. Completely enclosed in the house part, *free from all draught*, with food and water, the birds are greatly protected from night frights often caused by cats and other vermin. If a night light can be installed in the house, then protection from the effects of winter nights will be as complete as possible. Heating of course is desirable but, as explained earlier, this is really only vital for the half-hardy species, and many softbills will overwinter well without it if shut into adequate houses at night.

The house part should be large enough to accommodate all the aviary occupants and to enable the aviculturist to service them in reasonable comfort. It should be constructed of timber or brick and internally insulated by fixing hardboard or similar products on a minimum of a 3 cm square framework secured to the walls. The floor

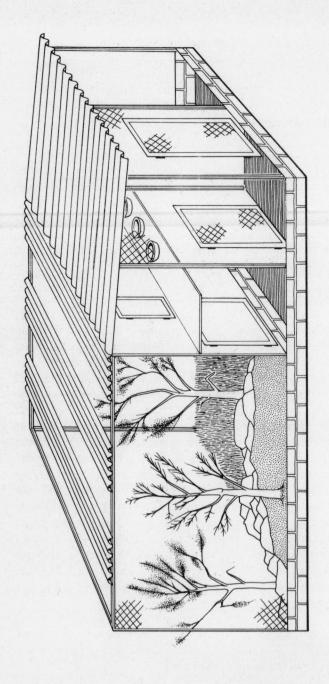

Figure 2 Recommended design for an outdoor softbill aviary. To show the inside more clearly, the exterior wall cladding has been omitted. Note the relative sizes of the doors in the safety porch, the 'stable doors' connecting the house part with the aviary flight, the feeding shelf and the corrugated PVC roofing

should be concrète which enables thorough cleaning and disinfection – certainly not earth or wood floor since they attract field mice. No windows are necessary, but if use is being made of an existing building which has windows, these should be double glazed. Heavy gauge polythene is acceptable but it must be firmly fixed. Even minute gaps will destroy the double glazing principle. Without windows the whole, or at least half, of the roof, should be covered with clear corrugated PVC sheeting or glass. Again, to prevent undue heat loss and eliminate draughts, a polythene false ceiling is recommended. Concrete should be pushed into the little half circles where the corrugated sheeting rests on the walls. Perching twigs must be provided. Instead of the impractical 'bob holes' traditionally provided as the means of entry for birds between house and flight, the 'stable door' principle is far more useful. Figure 3 illustrates this. The upper door approximately 30 cm wide by 90 cm high, is of solid wood and may be wedged fully open, half open, or whatever the weather conditions indicate. It is shut completely, with birds inside, as darkness approaches every winter night. Birds are not frightened of passing through, as they often are with bob holes – this is of major importance with new birds whose instincts tell them to avoid little holes leading into a dull house. The lower door, of similar height but twice the width, is for the owner's use, not the bird's. This is the owner's access to the flight. Initially it will be necessary to enter the flight each day to chase the birds inside, but it is surprising how quickly they learn the routine and are soon inside as daylight recedes, waiting for the door to be closed. This larger door can be made of solid wood also, but, to admit more light to the lower parts of the house, it could be made of a wooden frame with polythene covering both sides. If fitted with a night light, this should be quite dull and be switched on only during winter between say 3.30 p.m. and 8.00 a.m. When switching off each morning, the small (upper) door is opened and wedged in a position to suit the weather of the day, allowing the birds exercise in the flight during daylight hours. Food and drinking water should *always* be in the house part to encourage the softbills to enter and also to prevent contamination from wild birds' droppings falling through the flight roof.

A safety porch tall enough to stand in, with floor area of approximately one square metre, *must* be incorporated either inside or outside the house part. Daily use will be made of this when feeding and attending the collection. The door to enter the porch can be of conventional height and, once inside, the aviculturist must bolt it properly shut behind him. Then when entering the house part through the

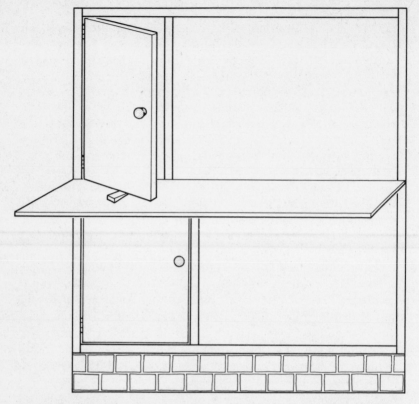

Figure 3 *Stable door principle, viewed from inside the house part of the aviary. Note the top door wedged in position according to weather conditions, the feeding shelf and the wider lower door for owner's use when entering the aviary flight*

opposite door – which should preferably be much lower – any bird escaping will only get as far as the inside of the safety porch.

Construction of the flight part of the aviary is of course basically of wire netting stretched over a timber framework. The wood must be at least 5 cm square, not necessarily planed as sawn timber is smooth enough, and then creosoted or painted. Placing the framework on the earth is not recommended because earth movement can damage the structure, the base timbers will quickly rot, and such aviaries are irresistible magnets to field mice and rats. A better result, and one much more attractive, comes from digging a small ditch, say 20 cm deep, filling it with broken bricks and concrete, then building either a single course of breezeblocks or 2 to 3 courses of bricks on top of this little foundation. The timber frame is then fixed upon that solid base. One absolutely vital job is to run small mesh wire netting about 20 cm down into the earth *outside* the flight and *immediately adjoining the base*, then turned outwards, *away* from the flight for about another 20 to 30 cms. Figure 4 illustrates this. The idea is that it prevents burrowing field mice – aviculture's number one enemy – from getting into the flight because they always start burrowing next to the aviary base. Other burrowing vermin should be similarly deterred. I have developed a method of stopping these tenacious little rodents from entering completely, but it is too costly for general application, so it comes down to making life as difficult as possible for burrowing rodents. It is for this reason also that I stressed food should always be in the house part. If properly built, this will be mouse-proof when the birds are shut into it at night – and this is when the rodents usually strike. They can of course easily gain entry into the flight, even with underground wiring, because they can climb as well as burrow. To combat climbing, the same corrugated PVC as used for roofing can be sawn into 30 cm horizontal strips and fixed to the *outside* of the flight, immediately *above* the brick base. The smooth horizontal corrugations make climbing impossible. With all these deterrents, if no food is in the flight, the effort is unrewarding to the outstandingly persistent mouse that does gain entry.

Instead of wire netting covering the *whole* of the flight, softbills benefit from the protection afforded by at least one side being solid. The direction of prevailing winds will determine which side should most advantageously be solid. Concerning wire netting, the fairly recent invention of welded square mesh netting has made aviary construction easier and more attractive. It is easy to work with and available in all kinds of mesh and gauge sizes. Each joint is welded and the finished product galvanized. Even the thinnest gauge should last longer than the conventional chicken wire and like all outdoor wire products, its life can be further extended by painting. Black is the most practical colour if this is contemplated.

The flight roof should be first covered with whatever wire mesh is being used for the whole job – then parts of it further covered with clear corrugated PVC sheeting or glass. Preferably each alternate 75 cm should be so covered – not just one half covered and the other half not. The idea is to allow rain on to the main growths of plants, yet provide adequate protection from heavy rain for the birds. In areas where cats are a problem, they must be deterred from getting on to the aviary roof. This is simply done by fixing a thin wood frame on 15 cm stilts on top of the actual roof, and stretching cheap, thin large-mesh chicken wire on this upper roof. Cats are reluctant to stand on anything not firm and which hampers a quick getaway. They will not walk ·on the chicken wire as it is thin and, though unlikely to cut their feet, is certainly uncomfortable. Similarly they will not step

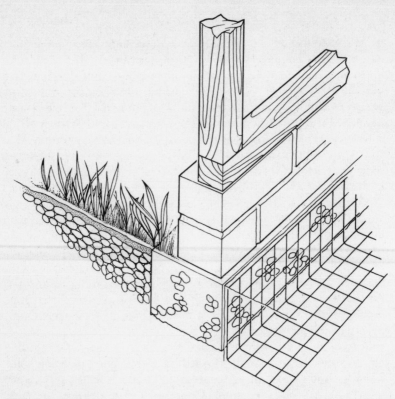

Figure 4 *Mouse-proofing for the aviary flight – wire netting underground turned away from the flight*

between each mesh as that would involve very high stepping and with each foot in a smallish hole, rapid escape would be impossible. Cats give up when they realize the risks of walking on such a roof. Costing nothing and just as effective, is covering the roof with boughs of gorse, rose or other thorny bush, but aesthetically this leaves a lot to be desired.

The internal landscaping of the flight is of course more exciting than building the aviary for most people and, once established, a variety of shrubs, a rockery and perhaps a *shallow* pool will blend into a very beautiful display. Until the shrubs reach the roof (when they must be topped) tree branches must be provided for perching in various places under the protected areas of the flight roof. The floor of the flight can either be grassed – though this will need periodical hand trimming – or covered with about 15 cm of peat mixed with earth. Another suitable mixture for the flight floor is equal parts of sand, earth and leaf-mould. A final alternative is the small stones sold by builder's merchants as pea shingle. Whichever floor covering is chosen, it, and any rockeries, must be cleaned at intervals. Exactly how often will depend on the number of softbills being kept and the nature of their droppings. Cleaning will involve collecting all loose droppings, raking the surface and possibly wiping some rocks. The usual source of ground infection in softbill flights – uneaten food particles which go mouldy – does not apply. This again is one of the many advantages of keeping the food in the concrete based house part as earlier stressed, which can be properly cleaned and disinfected whenever necessary. Such a system will enable the floor covering in the flight to remain for at least a year – probably much more – without any appreciable risk of ground infection. Even then it need not be actually replaced if thoroughly blow-lamped.

I have purposely avoided suggesting shrubs for the flight since local climatic conditions affect their selection. The best advice would be to talk to a local garden centre, or nurseryman, indicating that robust, fast-growing subjects are preferred.

Indoor aviaries

Outhouses, barns and similar buildings often lend themselves to use as indoor aviaries. Conversion is simple, being mostly a case of lining the building with smooth insulating board, inserting a false ceiling of similar material, wiring windows or double-glazing, resurfacing the floor to leave it smooth and cleanable. Excellent softbill accommo-dation can be produced by such conversions, the buildings often being large enough to divide into several aviaries both sides of a central corridor. Immediately inside the main door, a safety porch must be constructed, as with the outdoor aviary. Obvious advantages of such housing are that it should be virtually vermin proof and impossible for wild bird droppings to contaminate the contents.

An arrangement of natural branches for perching must be included in any indoor aviary, and the inclusion of some potted shrubs not only enhances the appearance but benefits the occupants. Peat-based floor covering is possible but will have to be replaced, due to contam-ination by food particles, twice a year.

Of course outdoor flights subject to there being enough ground, can be built out from the main building to provide the best of both worlds. In such instances, the building points covered under Outdoor aviaries apply.

Indoor aviaries in the literal sense of the word, have been created by town dwellers using a spare room of the house on numerous occasions. Subject only to a safety porch being built, and the wiring over of windows, this is a simple enough way of providing acceptable softbill accommodation.

Greenhouse/conservatory aviaries

For nectivorous softbills and hot lowland species of insectivores, this form of housing is ideal. The larger the better; it is possible to create a truly tropical environment, with authentic plant life and a virtually continuous breeding cycle of much livefood which cannot escape from such a building, when suitably adapted. It also forms the perfect winter accommodation for softbills not hardy enough to stay in outdoor aviaries all year round.

Atmospheric control within such buildings is difficult, humidity being perhaps the biggest problem. Unless proper double glazing is installed, condensation can become intolerable during cold weather, though fortunately it does not bother the birds. Nor are the plants disturbed – the warm, humid atmosphere encouraging remarkable growth in many varieties. Buildings such as these do not look right without a pool, but this too contributes to the humidity. Tropical plants rarely grow below 15°C, so this has to be the minimum temperature – though the birds themselves, when acclimatized, could stand five degrees less. During summer of course the problem is reversed. Sunlight on any area of glass soon increases the temperature below it enormously, but because of the warm outside temperature also, condensation does not occur. To humans at least the atmosphere is then more comfortable. Prolonged hot spells necessitate watering the plants and the peat-based floor covering.

The natural, though highly annoying, habit which many softbills have of flicking their food about, calls for frequent cleaning in any greenhouse/conservatory type aviary. There is no way of avoiding food particles souring as they land on the damp, soft floor and among the vegetation. It must therefore be a weekly job to remove them all, as far as is practical, and at the same time wiping any soiled leaves and rocks with a wet cloth. As with outdoor flights, the ground, when debris is removed, must be raked to maintain a fresh appearance. The closed and generally humid atmosphere necessitates the complete renewal of peat-based floor coverings, down to a depth of about 6 cms twice yearly. Care must be taken when so doing, not to unduly disturb the root systems of the major plants.

To dispel excess heat in hot weather and reduce the humidity at cooler times, ventilation is very important. An air vent near ground level at one corner and one near the ceiling in a diagonally opposite corner should help maintain a balanced atmosphere. Nevertheless, a row of manually operated adjustable ceiling windows, covered with fine mesh wire to prevent escapes (and wild birds getting in) will be necessary for hot weather.

For small softbills in particular, glass has many advantages over the various forms of wire netting – chiefly that the birds are easier to see, draughts are more or less excluded and contact with outside infection is less likely. Of great importance also is that all live insects so necessary to insectivores may be bred within the warm confines, and even when fully winged they will not be able to escape. Even during the hottest weather, when ceiling windows are open, insect escapes can be avoided if the wire netting is further covered with some form of cheesecloth or canvas. The warm, humid atmosphere, coupled with the ability to produce limitless insects make breeding success far more likely in these kind of aviaries. Apart from greater attention to cleanliness, the only real disadvantage they have is that if something happens to suddenly frighten the occupants, they may fly into the glass and hurt themselves. Fatalities have sometimes occurred as a result of such panics. Most aviculturists owning this type of aviary are prepared to take this fairly small risk, but the risk could be eliminated by painting countless tiny dots on the glass.

Tropical houses

What we have just described is in fact a miniature tropical house. Some zoos and one bird-garden in England have excellent tropical houses, which are large versions of the greenhouse/conservatory aviaries, displaying superb botanical collections with a wide variety of softbills which only live together because of the enormous space available. Larger species dominate the high regions, just as they would in the wild, whilst small chats, robins and the like which inhabit the forest's low secondary growth, flit happily around at eye level. Again, due to the space and amount of plant life, destructive softbills in relatively small numbers do no appreciable damage. Since flying insects cannot escape and hatch quickly, insectivores do well in tropical houses. This is particularly obvious with those which hawk flying insects and are therefore difficult avicultural subjects. Bee-eaters typify this fact.

Anyone contemplating building a greenhouse/conservatory type of aviary, or making a conversion from existing structures, should spend a few hours sitting in one of these proper tropical houses to gain ideas. It will be an enjoyable experience, and it is surprising what can be learned just by looking. With luck, a member of staff may also be available to answer any queries.

Heating

Any household heating methods are also suitable for birds, though in reality electricity, and to a lesser extent paraffin, are the only ones regularly used. Electric tubular heaters and oil-filled plug-in radiators are regularly employed in softbill rooms with success. Most are adjustable, and for ordinary electric fires it is possible to buy special plugs which incorporate thermostats. One or two electric heaters with these devices enable the heat to be regulated in a well-insulated room so that heaters come on and off automatically to maintain a pre-set temperature. For those acclimatized species receiving heat during winter, thermostats should be set at 8 to 12°C.

Paraffin heaters are often used in birdrooms and house parts of outdoor aviaries. It is claimed that with careful maintenance and religious weekly cleaning of the wicks, fumes are non-existent, and that no risk therefore applies. Whether greenhouse heaters, or the more sophisticated home types, all paraffin heaters must be used with the greatest care. It is one thing to have them in operation while you are there, but I would not feel happy with them left on unattended at nights. In an enclosed room, if they do begin to give off fumes, the results can be total loss. Birds are far more susceptible to dangerous fumes than humans (canaries were used in mines as 'early warning indicators' of gas for this very reason), and the fumes from an imperfectly adjusted paraffin heater are fatal. Certainly they are cheap to run, but the risk is high so the vastly more expensive, but safe, electricity has to be reluctantly recommended.

Where a birdroom is a room within the aviculturist's house, and the house has central heating, it is likely that the birdroom will have its own radiator. If so there is no heating problem as central heating is the ideal. A barn type building, converted to indoor aviaries, may be conveniently near the house, in which case central heating could possibly be extended to reach it. The capacity of the house boiler will have to be checked in that circumstance, to see if it is capable of supporting more radiators.

Wherever heating for birds is concerned, take the same care and precautions as you would in selecting your own domestic heating appliances. Seek expert advice if at all in doubt and, especially for night heating – on the grounds of simple safety – avoid any form of heating which involves naked flames.

5

Catching and handling

From time to time it is necessary to catch softbills for temporary removal to an exhibition, for example, or when a hitherto peaceful bird suddenly becomes aggressive, or when illness necessitates urgent transfer to the sick bay. Following the successful fledging of their offspring, some parent softbills are keen to produce a second clutch and will often bully the first youngsters; this is another typical occasion when catching and handling will be necessary.

Catching with a net

Catching and handling are simple enough operations in themselves but a definite knack is involved which, like all others, can only be developed with practice. Inexperience can cause undue panic among birds, as unsuccessful swiping with the net and much activity can so easily induce stress. Naturally it is easier to catch a bird from a cage than an aviary, but on all occasions the biggest 'Don't' to remember is don't rush wildly about swiping blindly with the net. This will panic all the birds, making many damage themselves by colliding with the wire netting. If the required bird is caught in such circumstances, it will be purely by luck. Calmness is the keynote.

If catching from an aviary, *all* movements should be fairly slow and purposeful – not one step being taken unnecessarily. It simplifies matters if a definite door, not just a hole, exists between the house part and the flight as with gentle arm movements, many unwanted birds can be chased into one part or the other, and the door closed. Having isolated the required bird, with as few others as possible, it will be seen that they all keep high (unless terrestrial species) and at the opposite end of the enclosure from where you are. Slowly advancing towards them with an arm stretched out will make them rapidly fly to the other end, again settling high. A couple of manoeuvres like that enables their movements to become predictable. It is thus possible to place them in the position most convenient for making the first (and hopefully the only) catching attempt. This is best done by advancing with arm outstretched, having learned where they are almost certain to head for, and holding the net in the other hand under the flight path. Then, while looking *only* at the bird required, quickly raise the net trying to catch that one bird in mid flight. Most aviary catching nets are about 25 to 30 cm diameter, which provides plenty of latitude when aiming for the usual size range of softbills.

Catching a bird in flight as it advances towards the net is preferable to the other method of taking aim while it is clinging to the wire netting, since too much force will harm, or even kill the bird, if it is accidentally struck by the rim of the net. Although padded, the rim is quite hard, and if the bird is not caught *within* the rim diameter, a definite risk exists. By moving as described, the birds do not become greatly panicked as they are allowed several escape routes. The method depends on predicting the bird's movements within the aviary, in relation to your own position. Then *only* use the net when you know where they will head, and when you are conveniently placed to make a strike. Check that the net will not become fouled on bushes and do not hesitate once you have calculated the moment for the strike. Admittedly it sounds difficult, but in the confines of an aviary it is possible with calculated manoeuvres to predict the bird's movements – the whole process having been made less confusing by the isolation of the required bird, with as few others as possible, initially.

Catching from cages

Catching a softbill from a cage is best done by hand, although in unusually long ones, a small aquarist's net may be of some value. Once more, learn the bird's movements. If the hand is placed inside the cage, in, say the back right corner, the bird will usually fly on to the cage front, in the top left – the farthest point away. It will remain there a few seconds if the hand is advanced towards it so, with a quick movement, it is possible to catch it before it moves elsewhere. Alternatively, it may be manoeuvred into a suitable position, as if catching from an aviary, before making the strike. Again, do not make repeated blind strikes – this will only cause exhaustion and great stress. Careful manoeuvring, making sure of an uninterrupted line of fire, then one quick accurate strike is the rule. Because of the confined space within a flight cage, it is not practical to catch birds in flight and, as they will invariably cling to the cage front, a quick strike with the cupped hand should secure them. Held against the cage front, the hand is then gently enclosed around the body, preventing wing movement but allowing the head freedom.

Catching from tropical houses

The removal of a specific bird from a large, heavily planted tropical house is far from easy. Baited trap cages, usually positioned with the benefit of earlier observation of the subject's habits, are normally resorted to. Great patience is required, and success is slow in coming. A mist net assembled in a suitable area is probably the best method, but has the enormous drawback in that it will catch most of the other occupants as well!

Handling

Having netted the required softbill from its aviary, or caught it by hand from a flight cage, its subsequent handling must be done with care to avoid the loss of feathers or perhaps injury. Holding any bird has to be done tightly enough to prevent escape or wriggling, but not so tight as to restrict normal breathing. Holding with insufficient pressure can allow a still bird to escape by suddenly and unexpectedly wriggling. Likewise, many birds will struggle continuously if not held firmly enough, dislodging numerous feathers in the process. When holding a bird, the head should never be enclosed, and ideally, the feet should be free, to avoid the possibility of them being held in an unnatural position. Fruit pigeons and chloropsis (fruitsuckers) are among those softbills whose feathers come out at the lightest touch, so extra special care is needed with them.

6
Diets and feeding techniques

Substitute or 'captive' diets are constantly being revised for softbills, as more of their natural food intake becomes known. Much of their natural diet consists of insects unobtainable outside their own countries and in non-tropical climates it is not possible to breed most insects in sufficient numbers to be of long-term help. Very recently crickets have been produced commercially and, although expensive, have proved of great value to softbill aviculturists who hitherto had to rely on maggots and mealworms for livefood, supplemented with whatever could be collected from the local countryside during warm weather. Locusts have also come on to the livefood market recently and are offered in a variety of sizes. This enables small ones ('hoppers') to be given to small softbills, while the hard, fully grown locusts are reserved for bigger species, such as shrikes, jays and magpies.

Many frugivores travel miles in search of the multitude of wild berries, as well as consuming large amounts of the more plentiful – and often cultivated fruits – like melons and bananas. Asiatic barbets have a strong preference for the various types of wild figs but these are among the many tropical fruits we cannot get.

So substitute diets are therefore based on what is known of the bird's natural diets, balanced against suitable alternative foods available here. This is well illustrated in the contents of the various commercially available insectile mixtures used by most softbill aviculturists. Hummingbird nutrition has been studied during the last decade, mainly in America, and proprietary nectar foods formulated for these birds have come as a result. With the addition of drosophila (tiny fruit flies which breed on decomposing fruit kept at 20 to 25°C) the more robust hummingbird species will thrive on these nectars. There still are, however, numerous hummingbirds from high altitudes and with more specialized feeding requirements, which have proved almost impossible to establish and these special preparations cannot be expected to overcome such difficulties.

Various softbill foods

Before describing tried and tested diets for each of the softbill groups, here is a checklist of the various foodstuffs. Concerning insectile mixtures and nectars, numerous recipes exist but they are all different ingredients; and the storage qualities of some are suspect. Mixtures which, in storage, are liable to become rancid or mouldy are obviously useless. So for safety, and to save time, I recommend buying one of the proprietary softbill (or insectile) mixtures which are well-balanced blends of foods containing proteins, carbohydrates, vitamins and minerals. If kept airtight, they remain moist and wholesome more or less indefinitely.

For a mixed collection of softbills, the following foodstuffs are required:

Fine grade insectile mixture – for small insectivores, omnivores and frugivores.

Coarse grade insectile mixture – for all larger species.

Nectar – one of the proprietary brands of nectar powders which are diluted, with sugar, in warm water as maker's instructions. The resultant liquid (artificial nectar) is suitable for hummingbirds but as other nectivores use less energy, their nectar can be made with honey instead of sugar. Honey does not have so many carbohydrates as sugar so, when eaten, provides less energy.

Fruit – all and every type providing it is ripe and soft. Whilst some softbills such as tanagers and starlings will peck mouthfuls of fruit from rough-cut chunks or slices, most pick up and swallow small pieces whole. This comes from their natural food, mainly berries, which are plucked and swallowed whole. For this reason fruit given in captivity, being large cultivated varieties, must be chopped into small dices of between ½ and 1 cm. All captive softbills prefer their fruit this way.

Softbill aviculturists sometimes omit oranges from their bird's diets, on the grounds that they have a scouring effect. Oranges, however, are well known to contain the important vitamin C and, for frugivores especially, whose diet is devoid of several important vitamins, this should not be deliberately witheld. Bananas have likewise come in for criticism – it being said that they are overfattening, but enormous amounts have to be fed over long periods before such effects occur. Conversely, soaked dried grocer's fruit (sultanas, currants, apricots etc) are usually considered perfect for frugivores and fed in disproportionate amounts. These are in fact more fattening than bananas. As with all things, *moderation* should be the keynote. No fruit should be overfed and none purposely witheld. A good mixture should be aimed for although seasonal shortages of certain fruits occasionally make this difficult. Harmful chemical changes take place when fruit is over-ripe so although such 'bargains' as sleepy pears, which look all right outwardly but are largely rotten pulp within, may be offered, do not use them.

Maggots – these must be kept in an open-top container in bran for three days so that they can clean themselves both internally and externally. They will empty the gut of the black spot of decomposed meat, on which they have been bred. Immediately the first chrysalis is seen, change the bran since, if this part of their life cycle takes place in the old bran, now contaminated, harmful bacteria will develop. By keeping in *cool* temperatures, their life cycle is slower but do *not* keep maggots in a refrigerator as that degree of coldness will stop them cleaning themselves.

Blowflies – a few jars with perforated lids should contain some maggot chrysalis, when cleaned, in either bran or sand for hatching into blowflies. If a jar without its lid is placed in a softbill cage or aviary, the flies will be eaten as they emerge and before their wings have grown.

Mealworms – stored in bran, which they eat, these are possibly the most valuable livefood, and may be bred. However, the process is long and unlikely to yield sufficient worms. Bought commercially they will keep many weeks and, like the maggot, are good softbill food during *any* stage of their cycle.

Locusts and/or crickets – use fairly quickly but to be regarded as an extra, whereas the above three livefoods are basics.

Raw minced meat – whilst raw minced beef or beefheart are usually recommended, chicken and lamb are good also. I regularly use mixed raw minced meat which, if minced finely, is appreciated by almost all softbills.

Hard-boiled egg – either mashed or chopped very finely this food though considered indigestible, is of the utmost importance in captive softbill diets.

Cheese – a high-fat food, greatly recommended but only used in small amounts. Its main use comes as a provider of the vital extra fat needed by softbills overwintering outdoors.

Stale bread and/or spongecake – when moistened with nectar or milk, and crumbled into small pieces, this is of course high in energy-producing carbohydrates and, due to its palatability, seems universally acceptable among softbills.

Dead day-old chicks, mice and chunks of raw beef – these items are mostly needed for carnivorous softbills which do not feature in most softbill collections, though they form a *part* of the diets of crow-like birds (*corvidae*) within the omnivores group.

Shrimps, whitebait, sprats – wading birds live largely on these items plus raw minced meat and hard-boiled eggs, and other things in smaller quantities. However, waders are also rarely seen outside zoos; but for the sake of completeness, these foods must be included in the softbill's diet check list. Even so, I have known shrimps to be eaten by certain frugivores and omnivores, so there is no reason why they may not be used as an occasional extra.

Diet for omnivores

Unfortunately this group must be divided into those fairly near to insectivores who require more animal protein and solid foods generally; and the other omnivorous softbills whose diet leans towards that of frugivores – i.e. fruit forms the major part of their food.

Omnivores in the first section include mynahs, starlings, jays, drongoe, orioles, robins, sivas, mesias, babblers, Asiatic cuckoos, thrushes, ground thrushes, coucals, troupials, marshbirds, mockingbirds, treepies, glossy starlings.

Diet: 40% fruit, 10% raw minced meat, 10% soaked bread and/or spongecake, 30% coarse insectile mixture, 10% livefood. All items mixed together and, though not vital, any surplus hard-boiled egg will be welcomed.

Omnivores comprising the second section are those requiring larger proportions of fruit. Typical members of this section are cotingas including cocks-of-the-rock, barbets, lesser green broadbills (but not other broadbills which are highly insectivorous and unfortunately rare in aviculture), African bulbuls, Asiatic bulbuls, manakins, toucans, fairy bluebirds, fruitsuckers, and the enormous family of tanagers, including their allied species euphonias and chlorophonias.

Diet: 65% fruit, 10% raw minced meat, 10% soaked bread and/or spongecake, 10% coarse insectile mixture, 5% livefood. All items mixed together. Extras to the standard diet should be confined to the occasional dish of nectar.

Diet for frugivores

As well as diced fruit, certain vegetables may be boiled and mixed with it. Potatoes, carrots and swedes are those regularly used. The only point in their favour is that probably additional vitamins and, in the case of potatoes, carbohydrates, will enrich the diet. Every week I dust the frugivores' food with nectar powder to ensure they receive adequate protein, vitamins and minerals because fruit itself is insufficient.

There are many frugivores; the main ones available to aviculture include mousebirds (or colies), cedar waxwings, fruit pigeons and touracos. It can be argued that fruitsuckers and most of the 'fruit-biased' omnivores should appear here, but they would all suffer from malnutrition if maintained purely on fruit for very long. True frugivores seem to thrive on a fruit-only diet, although it must be admitted that they consume livefood readily enough – markedly so when rearing young.

Diet: 80% fruit, 10% raw minced meat, 10% coarse grade insectile mixture or the soaked bread; all mixed together. It is pointless using more than 10% insectile mixture since they will often refuse food altogether if the fruit has been too heavily laced with other things. The tiny particles of insectile food stick well to the diced fruit, of course, so it is easy to get into them the modest amounts they will tolerate.

Diet for hummingbirds and sunbirds

The minute fruit flies known as drosophila are essential if hummingbirds and sunbirds are being maintained. They are eaten with varying degrees of enthusiasm by other nectivores. Small mealworms and freshly hatched blowflies are the more usual livefoods for them. Kept out of bright light, over-ripe fruit (preferably bananas) will soon attract drosophila in summer. If it is then kept where the temperature varies between 20 and 26°C for the rest of the year, a culture of these small flies should be formed. Once in during the summer, they lay eggs on the fruit and their life cycle rapidly begins. The fruit should be reasonably dry so citrus fruits are not so useful as bananas. Fruit in jars, with perforated lids, provides drosophila conveniently in bird-rooms, but a more productive 'manure heap' can be discreetly formed behind plants in a greenhouse type aviary or tropical house. The smell is not offensive and blends well with the damp botanical odour unavoidable in such houses.

Nectivores, as well as the obvious hummingbirds and sunbirds, include honeycreepers, Asiatic flowerpeckers, South American flowerpiercers, spiderhunters, Asiatic white eyes (zosterops), African white eyes (zosterops) and banana quits. *Small diet variations apply as follows:*

Diet for hummingbirds: Mainly nectar, making the liquid from one of the commercially available high-protein powders and sugar. This is fed in a glass or plastic feeding tube which resembles a 12 cm long test-tube with red drinking spout pointing upwards from the base, and filling cap at the top. Such tubes are commercially available and *must* be thoroughly washed each day before being refilled with new nectar. At least one tube for each bird, they are hung in various positions so that the hummingbirds can drink while hovering. Other drinking containers are generally shunned, although a flat bottle with an upward facing hole, painted red around their edge (hummingbirds are always attracted to red) are favoured by the sicklebill species. Nectar, plus literally as many drosophila as possible, form the standard captive hummingbird diet.

Some species are much more insectivorous than others, but all of them require, proportionate to their size, lots of drosophila. In times of shortage, suitable animal protein can be added to the nectar in the form of one of the proprietary beef extracts, but this provides no bulk and is not a long-term substitute for drosophila. Some aviculturists make a less rich nectar to carry the birds through the night, but there is little point in this as hummingbirds regularly go torpid (a condition similar to hibernation) when sleeping. Torpidity may not occur if night temperatures are the same as daytime, since the condition is associated with reduced temperatures. In such cases, the normal nectar will suffice and a dim night light is recommended.

Diet for sunbirds: This is the same nectar as hummingbirds have but, as mentioned earlier, nothing burns energy like hummingbirds and so there is sense in substituting honey for sugar when making sunbird's nectar. However, the point is open to argument and my own opinion is that honey need only be used in place of sugar where sunbirds are housed in cages. Excess energy produced from a sugar-based nectar should be worked off where ample exercising space exists. In any event, hummingbirds and sunbirds are regularly housed together in tropical houses where, even if a variety of nectars were available, there can be no control over who eats what.

Sunbirds, particularly when caged, take their nectar happily from a small dish on the floor, so tubes are only vital for hummingbirds. A chunk of bread and/or spongecake is placed in the dish also as most sunbirds develop a taste for this valuable food. The Asiatic species are also quite frugivorous, and so I offer fruit in a separate dish for all sunbirds.

Livefood is important and whilst drosophila are eaten by most, particularly the smaller species, newly-hatched blowflies, or the smaller housefly of any age, are more appropriate. Malachite, scarlet-chested and bronzy are among the larger African species which eat mealworms readily also.

Diet for all other nectivores

The wide variety of birds within this group means that certain species will pick out particular foods, but to specify percentages of foods for every species would only be of academic interest. By offering an acceptable mixture, species will select quantities of each food according to their natural needs and instincts. The foods are always given in dishes placed on the floor, or on a rock in tropical houses. No need for nectar tubes.

Diet: 60% nectar, 25% fruit, 10% bread and/or spongecake, 5% raw minced meat. In *another* dish equal parts of fine-grade insectile mixture and livefood are placed. Insectile mixture is hardly ever taken by choice so the insects are rolled in stiff nectar to make them sticky. A little of the insectile mixture is then bound to adhere to them, forcing the birds to eat some of it. Whilst maggots may be rolled in moist things and still live, mealworms quickly die if their heads are not kept dry, so if doing this job with mealworms, hold their heads to prevent contact with anything fluid. The reason for giving dry foods separately is that they lose their palatability if added to a larger volume of nectar. Insectile mixtures are not vital to nectivores, so the fact that they do not eat much of them need not cause concern. The jars of flies are of much greater importance to them and should never be overlooked.

Diet for insectivores

As the name suggests, insects form the natural diet of these birds, and the aviculturist is hard pressed in providing insects in sufficient variety to prevent malnutrition, which inevitably occurs when nothing but maggots and mealworms are fed over a long period. This is why the acceptance of inanimate foods – i.e. a fairly well-balanced diet – is of the utmost importance.

During the summer months, all dedicated softbill keepers take to the countryside with various devices for collecting wild insects. These are enormously valuable for insectivorous softbills since they not only correspond to the natural diet, but contain a larger variety of nutrients – as well as providing a welcome change to commercial insects. One method of collecting commonly used is to place an up-turned umbrella under a bush and then beat the bush. Spiders, caterpillars, and all sorts of useful creatures fall into the umbrella, which must then be quickly closed and knocked out over a large jar.

'Meating-off', the art of getting insectivores to take inanimate foods, requires patience and a number of tricks. The business of coating insects in a sticky food and then putting them into insectile mixture is done frequently. Any insect can be coated with stiff nectar or honey to make them sticky (and incidentally adding much goodness), but their heads must be left clean, or they will soon die. Only maggots will survive complete coating. The theory is that while eating living insects exclusively, the fact that they have been 'doctored' will force the birds into accepting the taste of insectile mixture, and so be more likely to eat the mixture alone eventually. It does work, but takes a long time. Naturally, the process is most demanding when dealing with such species as flycatchers and bee-eaters who catch insects on the wing. Maggots and mealworms are not much help initially with these, but crickets and blowflies can be coated and tossed individually towards the birds. Very few are eaten at first so they are all collected, recoated, and tossed again. The process is tedious but capable of rapid improvement if a 'teacher' is available. That is an established bird of same or related species, and the new birds follow the teacher's feeding habits. Of necessity, most insectivorous softbills receive an unbalanced diet comprising commercial insects only until the meating-off is well under way. At that stage, the presence of pellets indicates that the digestive system is functioning properly and that adequate roughage is in the diet.

It is important that insectivores learn to eat hard-boiled egg and raw minced meat. The former, rather surprisingly, is often taken early in the meating-off process. I think it is because, if chopped in tiny bits, the egg resembles live ant eggs which are sometimes used for insectivore feeding in tropical countries, but which we cannot obtain commercially here. Minced meat given in a lump is unattractive to insectivores – established birds often failing to touch it – so it must be separated into the smallest particles. Small pellets of raw minced meat, dusted with insectile mixture, and tossed individually to blue rollers, dollar birds, motmots etc., have often been used to meat-off such large insectivores.

Flycatchers, chats, minivets, magpie robins, shamas, rock thrushes, rubythroats, wagtails, tits, woodpeckers, motmots, pittas, nuthatches and robins are among the more readily available insectivores.

Diet: 30% insectile mixture, 15% mashed or finely chopped hard-boiled egg, 15% raw minced meat, 20% maggots and chrysalis, 15% mealworms, 2½% grated or finely chopped cheese, 2½% grated carrot. Everything is mixed together, but the egg and meat sprinkled on the top since these items quickly become unattractive if swamped with a greater volume of insectile mixture. Crickets and locusts are best handed out more or less individually, selecting the most suitable sized ones for each softbill. Waste of these expensive insects is eliminated this way, and such occasions help in taming the birds. Jars of hatching blowflies are provided always, and replaced with new ones as they become eaten.

Diet for carnivores

The African bush shrikes and small Asiatic shrikes fall more into the insectivores group, but most shrikes are carnivorous. Hornbills, though more accurately classed as omnivores, are very highly carnivorous, and the Abyssinian ground hornbill completely so. Several terrestrial North American large softbills, like the groove-billed anis, though rarely seen in aviculture, are plainly carnivorous, and the forest kingfishers feature strongly in this softbill group also. Perhaps the familiar zoological exhibit, the kookaburra, is the most well known of the kingfishers who do not fish. Instead they live on lizards, snakes, mice and the like. The carnivores are a robust group of softbills, generally hardy, and requiring simple diets. Shrikes, hunting cissas and others will live satisfactorily in modest aviaries, but the majority are big birds and consequently require more space. Although mainly zoological birds, any private softbill aviculturist with suitable accommodation would find little difficulty in maintaining this group in good order.

Diet: 45% raw meat cut into lengths approximately 7 cm by 1 cm and rubbed hard into insectile mixture, so that it not only adheres to the meat but penetrates the surface; 45% dead day-old chicks which are obtainable commercially, 10% dead mice. Mice are bred for laboratory use, but of course any mice obtained from a pet shop will quickly multiply, providing the relatively small number required on a regular basis. All these items to be dusted with nectar powder or veterinary mineral mixes at least once weekly. Large locusts are much appreciated and usually given as extras.

Sprats, whitebait and shrimps (chopped up where necessary) are all taken by the various forest kingfishers if placed in a large dish of shallow water, but these birds, although locally common, are becoming avicultural rarities.

Daily routines and hygiene

In feeding softbills, careful attention must always be paid to hygiene. All foods, apart from insectile mixtures, are perishable and *must* be prepared fresh daily. It is possible to prepare egg, for example, in bulk and store in a refrigerator. However, the bulk must be cooled before going in the refrigerator or salmonella can develop, and daily rations must be left out long enough to reach room temperature prior to feeding. Consumption of freezing cold food is dangerous to tropical softbills – and most other creatures. In practice such precautions are rarely taken. Very little extra time is needed to prepare all foods fresh daily, which will be nutritionally better and safer. All uneaten food from the previous day *must* be destroyed. In aviaries, it will be necessary to sweep up scattered food particles. In cages, the paper is usually changed, removing old food particles in the process.

In maintaining a large and varied collection, the development of a logical routine is essential if one is not to go bonkers! This involves preparing all foodstuffs *before* starting feeding, and having an additional set of dishes, tubes or whatever else is necessary. Only then can feeding begin. Filling dishes with the correct foods, it is a simple matter to put them on to a tray or trolley and deliver to the cages or aviaries – collecting the old ones at the same time. The pile of old dishes are then taken back to the kitchen, their contents destroyed and the dishes thoroughly washed and stacked ready for the next day. By using two sets of dishes instead of washing-up as you go, tremendous time is saved. The feeding routine will no doubt differ from one collection to another but in the interests of efficiency a logical routine must be developed.

Dishes

The size of dishes obviously depends on how many birds take their food from them, but in mixed collections, several smaller dishes well spaced out are far better than one big dish. This prevents the dominant bird from guarding the food and stopping other birds from feeding. Maggots and mealworms quickly wriggle to the bottom of food dishes and so will be unobtainable until the birds eat most of the inanimate foods – or when this fact is discovered the birds will annoyingly scatter the food to reach the livefood. For these reasons shallow dishes offering a fairly large surface area are preferable. It is also important that dishes be dry because otherwise maggots and mealworms can climb out. Plastic dishes are perfectly suitable for softbill feeding, though not so long-lasting as stainless steel, which are best. Both have a serious disadvantage where heavy softbills are concerned because their weight can topple the dishes over if they stand on the edges. For these types, thick china, earthenware or glass dishes must be used.

7

Breeding

Existing accommodation will largely dictate what softbill breeding could be attempted as aviary furnishings will differ considerably from one species to another. However, there are several golden rules which apply to softbill breeding – all of equal importance.

1. The flights of softbill breeding aviaries must be well planted. Thick bushes, even young trees, climbers and ground-covering plants all attract insects and provide nesting sites, together with that vital privacy. No softbill is likely to breed if privacy is not afforded. With the aid of advice from the local garden centre, fast-growing plants may be selected which should give adequate cover after one year of growth. The range is limited, the majority of shrubs needing more time to grow sufficiently. Invariably softbill breeding success occurs in heavily planted aviaries where birds have built their own nests in the vegetation, as distinct from using artificial nesting baskets or boxes.

2. Although compatible collections of softbills are common, fighting often develops as they reach breeding condition and become keen on claiming a territory. Serious aviculturists will therefore house each potential breeding pair separately. A block of planted aviaries can cover the same ground as one large structure, but naturally costs more for the extra materials. Housing each pair individually stops the competition for livefood so, with the aviculturist helping provide more insects, it is likely that a pair could successfully rear young.

3. If young hatch, livefood will be required in large amounts, and it is to attract and produce insects that an aviary compost heap is so valuable. The smaller softbills are helped greatly by this, as it yields numerous very tiny insects. A proper compost heap is neither smelly nor unsightly, but it can easily be sited behind shrubs to make its presence less obvious. Small examples of the commercially available livefoods, dusted with nectar powder and crushed calcium tablets, are also necessary. With these two sources of livefood, and no other birds taking any, parent birds stand a good chance of successful rearing.

The aviculturist must further assist by providing a regular supply of the jars containing blowfly hatchlings. These will quickly be caught as they emerge, soft and wingless, from the jars and their nutritional value is far higher than maggots or mealworms. The collection of wild insects using the umbrella technique or some other method must also be a regular chore.

4. It may seem obvious, but sexually identical softbills may not in fact be a pair. Buying four birds instead of just two is recommended in these instances, as from four a pair should emerge.

5. Any pair must be compatible. Breeding is unlikely if a couple cannot stand each other. Further purchases or preferably exchanges should rectify this problem.

6. Both cock and hen *must* be in full breeding condition. This means literally bubbling with health and vigour. Cocks usually reach breeding condition first but if the hen is nowhere near ready, it is best to remove the cock until the hen *is* completely in condition. This prevents the cock attacking his mate, which he may do if she does not respond to his courtship. This invariably happens if she is not in full breeding condition.

Helping the breeding pair

Following these golden rules will maximize breeding potential, but with softbill breeding there is no parallel with budgerigar or canary breeding where results can be fairly accurately predicted in capable hands. This is because softbills are wild birds, not domesticated, and when breeding generally shun close association with man – even though they may be quite bold at other times. A 'partnership' between the breeding pair and owner must however exist in the supply of livefood. The average aviary, even with insect-attracting plants and a compost heap, will not yield enough livefood for successful rearing, without the help of the aviculturist. Human interference, during breeding, must never extend beyond the supply of livefood. Certainly no attempt to close-ring chicks should be made, as this massive interference will almost certainly lead to desertion. Some dedicated softbill aviculturists visit the countryside where ant nests exist. They dig out sections containing numerous ant eggs. These, while fresh, have a high nutritional content and the religious collection of them each evening has been largely responsible for several notable breeding successes. This form of livefood, as well as aphis, is very valuable for small species of breeding softbills especially. The inclusion of a few roses in the aviary will usually guarantee a plentiful supply of aphis.

The ideal is to try to discover the bird's natural habitat and plant the breeding aviary specifically to correspond. This also includes aviary furnishings – tree stumps, rocks, pools, sandy floors, peat floors etc.

Not surprisingly, softbills whose chicks are big enough to manage maggots and small mealworms from an early age breed more successfully in captivity than very tiny species – the chicks of whom require quite minute insects initially. This is largely the reason for starling specialization among a few softbill enthusiasts, and why that family breed regularly in certain zoos and bird gardens.

Breeding by controlled liberty

One very successful method of breeding softbills, especially the smaller and more demanding species, is to allow controlled liberty until just before the young fledge. If this method is to be adopted, a small trap door on the flight roof, or on the front fairly high up, should be made before the breeding season begins. In the case of new aviaries, such a door can be incorporated in the design and included as part of the building job.

The pair are confined to their aviary until the first egg is due to hatch, then the trap door is opened. The theory is that the parents will roam the vicinity collecting the insects naturally, returning to incubate and feed their babies much as they would do in the wild, invariably sleeping in the aviary themselves – drawn by routine, the presence of their offspring and plentiful food (adult softbill diet). It is of course *vital* to permanently close the trap door a day or two before the chicks are due to leave the nest, choosing a moment when both parents are inside the aviary, which is likely to be late evening.

There are obvious risks involved. What if one or both parents desert? They may be lost for ever. It is unsafe to use the method if cats or other predators frequent the vicinity – and it is not recommended if accurate dates are not known because if anticipated fledging dates are misjudged, the whole family may disappear. Finally, the method only applies where a breeding pair are the *sole* occupants of an aviary, because other birds would not be subject to the same restraints.

Nevertheless, in quiet areas not inhabited by cats, and where birds of prey are no problem, the method can be very successful and of course it relieves the aviculturist of the tedium of insect-collecting.

Nesting materials and receptacles

Plenty of nesting material (hay, old downy feathers, artificial or natural hair, short lengths of wool and string etc.) must be scattered around the aviary, so that those who wish to build their own nest in a bush can do so. A small area of mud – maybe allowing the aviary pool to overflow – is appreciated by many softbills as an aid to nestbuilding. The nesting materials will also be collected by other softbills who prefer making a concave within one of the nesting baskets or boxes which should be provided to encourage breeding. Figure 5 illustrates typical examples of nesting boxes and baskets. They are not marketed for softbills in particular, but captive birds generally. The baskets are sometimes favoured by small babblers and tanagers, while hole-nesting species such as tits make regular use of nesting boxes. The boxes are of course easy to make, and so the proportions can be varied according to the species involved. Starlings and mynahs, reliable breeders when established, sometimes prefer taller nesting boxes, such as the conventional parakeet boxes, but in any softbill aviary several nesting receptacles of different shapes and sizes should be provided so that a pair's preference can be discovered. When the choice has been made, it is usual to just rehang that one for subsequent breeding seasons since it is conceivable that surplus boxes and baskets could be taken over by mice.

Old blackbird and thrush nests are well worth collecting at the end of each summer. These can be stored until the following spring and then placed in suitable forks among the aviary bushes. Being natural, instead of man-made, they sometimes stimulate breeding activities among captive softbills of related kinds.

Hand-rearing softbills

Night-frights, cats and other vermin, interference by an understandably curious owner – these and many more things can cause unexpected desertion of the nest. If only eggs are in the nest, there is nothing to be done since artificial incubation of softbill eggs is a subject for which virtually no data exists. If young are in the nest and if the desertion is discovered before they perish, hand-rearing is worth trying. To stand a reasonable chance of success, the chicks need to be over a week old as newly hatched chicks are exceedingly difficult unless one is well experienced in hand-rearing, and can attend to them virtually as a full-time job.

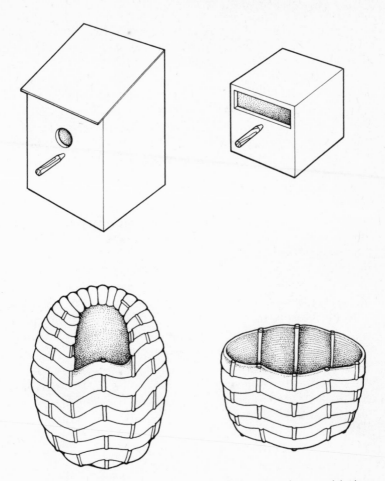

Figure 5 *Typical examples of commercially available nesting boxes and baskets*

Chicks should be put into a hospital cage set at 34°C, or a stout box fitted with overhead light. The latter has the disadvantage that, providing constant brilliant light, the chicks are never at complete ease. Furthermore, the temperature cannot be accurately regulated. A bottle of water, minus lid, should stand in one corner to provide the necessary humidity. The chicks should be contained in a soft concave of their original nest size, within the hospital cage or heated box. A flower pot saucer lined with soft tissues, which must be renewed daily, serves this purpose well. Very young chicks should be fed every hour between about 5.00 a.m. and midnight – that is why, combined with the awkwardness of handling such small creatures, they are so difficult. After a week, however, feeding can be every 1½ hours, then reduced to every 2 hours a few days later.

Many recipes exist for rearing foods, but a suitable mixture can be made from any good baby cereal food, plus about 10% each of meat extract, nectar powder, and the contents of mealworms (the worm minus its skin). A powderized calcium tablet is added to every alternate feed. These items are all mixed with warm milk to a creamy consistency. The temperature of the food should be between 30 and 36°C, not cooler. Feeding is done with a small syringe, with about 3 cm of very thin plastic tube pressed over its nozzle. Both of these can be supplied by local veterinary surgeons and, if kept scrupulously clean, will last indefinitely. By holding the chick and tapping its beak with the loaded syringe, he will quickly gape for food. The tube is then inserted *over* the tongue and a little food syringed down the throat into the crop. This will soon fill as more food is consumed and, when it looks rounded or stops gaping, enough food will have been consumed for that feed. Keep the food hot or the chick will refuse it – fooling you into thinking he has had enough when he has not.

Longer periods between feeds, plus a coarser mixture, will be all right as the chick grows, and when past the very baby stage feeding times can be gauged very easily by their cheeping. The temperature must also be gradually reduced as the chick grows and when he is feathered a normal room temperature will be adequate. One difficulty with hand-rearing is getting the bird on to the usual adult food when he has reached fledging stage, and indeed most are reluctant to even feed themselves. It is at that point that the introduction of another bird (of as similar species as possible) can advantageously be tried. If caged next to the fledgling, learning by example usually soon follows, saving the aviculturist a long and very trying job.

Due to their close association with humans, hand-reared softbills are always very tame, which is perhaps the chief reward to the aviculturist. When such birds mature, contrary to popular belief, they *do* make good parents because they will accept far more help from the aviculturist than a wild-caught softbill, and not be nervous of him.

A question may come to mind at this stage: why is livefood so important for natural rearing when it is hardly used in hand-rearing? The answer is that softbills' instincts tell them that their young must receive live insects. If their instincts allowed them to feed their chicks with artificial concoctions provided by the aviculturist, healthy chicks would be reared just the same.

Black-chinned yuhina
(*Yuhina nigrimenta*)

Yellow-naped yuhina
(*Yuhina flavicollis*)

Indian blue roller
(*Coracias benghalensis*)

Red-billed hornbill
(*Tokus erythrorhynchus rufirostris*)

Southern pied hornbill
(*Anthracoceros convexus*)

Verditer flycatcher
(*Muscicapa thalassina*)

Black-throated wattle eye
(*Platysteira peltata*)

Thick-billed euphonia
(*Euphonia laniirostris*)

Blue-naped chlorophonia
(*Chlorophonia cyanea*)

Fire-headed barbet, Male
(*Capito bourcierii*)

Fire-headed barbet, Female
(*Capito bourcierii*)

Gaudy barbet
(*Megalaima mystacophanos*)

Red-plumed bird of paradise
(*Paradisaea apoda raggiana*)

Red-whiskered bulbul
(*Pycnonotus jocosus*)

Red-bearded bee-eater
(*Nyctyornis amictus*)

Blue-bearded bee-eater
(*Nyctyornis athertoni*)

European bee-eater
(*Merops apiaster*)

Toco toucan
(*Ramphastos toco*)

Sulphur-breasted toucan
(*Ramphastos sulphuratus*)

Lesser green broadbill
(*Calyptomena viridis*)

Black-faced dacnis
(*Dacnis lineata*)

Yellow-collared honeycreeper
(*Iridophanes pulcherrima*)

Banana quit
(*Coereba flaveola*)

Spectacled spiderhunter
(*Arachnothera flavigaster*)

Stork-billed kingfisher
(*Pelargopsis capensis*)

Red-headed tit
(*Aegithalos concinnus*)

Red-capped manakin
(*Pipra mentalis*)

Quetzal
(*Pharomachrus mocinno*)

Golden-fronted fruitsucker
(*Chloropsis aurifrons*)

Blue-winged fruitsucker
(*Chloropsis cochinchinensis*)

Asian fairy bluebird
(*Irena puella*)

Troupial
(*Icterus icterus*)

Thick-billed fruit pigeon
(*Treron curvirostra*)

Vinous-throated parrotbill
(*Paradoxornis webbiana*)

Giant pitta
(*Pitta caerulea*)

Gurney's pitta
(*Pitta gurneyi*)

Sunbittern
(*Eurypyga helias*)

Cedar waxwing
(*Bombycilla cedrorum*)

Indian white eye
(*Zosterops palpabrosa*)

Royal starling
(*Cosmopsarus regius*)

Rothschild's mynah
(*Leucopsar rothschildi*)

Golden-crested mynah
(*Mino coronatus*)

Paradise tanager
(*Tangara chilensis*)

Spangled tanager
(*Tangara nigroviridis*)

Golden-eared tanager
(*Tangara chrysotis*)

Flame–faced tanager
(*Tangara parzudakii*)

Orange–eared tanager
(*Chlorochrysa calliparaea*)

Magpie tanager
(*Cissopis leveriana*)

Luck is important

Breeding softbills, as with all non-domestic livestock, requires a good measure of luck. I once knew a man who happened to have a pair of pekin robins among his nondescript finch and canary collection. They lived largely on seed and canary softfood, but received uncleaned maggots when he noticed that they had eggs in a canary nestpan! Against all aviculturist principles, a single healthy chick was raised – by luck rather than good husbandry. Another pair of the same birds, housed magnificently in an aviary belonging to a very dedicated aviculturist and with the finest diet possible, produced fertile eggs but took no further interest. That gentleman *deserved* breeding success. The first one certainly did not but was simply lucky. This little story illustrates the importance of luck when all other ingredients have been put into the avicultural pot. The most experienced aviculturist in the world will achieve little without it. Too many factors remain outside his control for it to be otherwise, and in some avicultural circles, only limited credit is given for a breeding success unless it can be repeated for several generations.

8
Exhibiting

Conservationists and the anti-birdkeeping lobby – ill-informed and lacking in practical knowledge of the subject as they are – regularly criticize bird exhibitions. The relatively cramped conditions of some showcages (not softbills' showcages), coupled with the exposure of the birds to continual human activity, are the major arguments against these events, so can exhibiting be humanely justified? Generally the answer is yes, but not for known highly strung species or individual birds of nervous disposition. The vast majority of entries are always domesticated varieties of cage and aviary birds anyway, which are unaffected by the activity within the exhibition hall.

It must be emphasized that only established and acclimatized softbills are exhibited, since newly imported birds, fresh out of quarantine, will not have 100 per cent perfect plumage and so would not do well in competition. Neither will they have developed enough tolerance of humans within that period to behave steadily in the showcage. To win at exhibitions, birds must be steady as well as physically perfect. Experienced softbill aviculturists do not exhibit any bird until at least a year after purchase. During that time, the bird will have moulted out and grown a theoretically perfect set of new feathers, and become very accustomed to human activity. In such circumstances, only very minimal stress will be caused by entering in the *occasional* exhibition – indeed many softbills regularly seen at exhibitions genuinely seem to enjoy their outings.

Bird exhibitions are desirable in that they increase or arouse public interest in aviculture; and softbills are usually responsible for providing the most spectacular exhibits. Many visitors have their initial interest in the subject sparked off by visiting an exhibition. The National Exhibition of Cage and Aviary Birds, held each December at Alexandra Palace in London, is the biggest exhibition. This, together with other major exhibitions are of great importance to international aviculturists, who travel from many countries to meet and talk in depth. No other events provide meeting places for far-flung aviculturists against a background of living birds. The exchange of knowledge and comparison of experiences are of benefit to all. Finally, exhibitions develop enthusiasm and add to the knowledge of the younger generation of aviculturists. They learn much by talking to owners of winning exhibits and the experts who always frequent such events. Also, they can take part in the juvenile classes where their own birds may be entered and compete against those of other youngsters.

Preparing for exhibitions

Since the breeding season is restricted to the summer months, exhibitions take place mostly during the winter. Entering a bird in an exhibition *occasionally* should not reduce its breeding potential as it will have at least three months to readjust to normal conditions between the last exhibition and the advent of the breeding season. Smaller softbills whose winter arrangements involve removal to heated quarters may perhaps experience one or two exhibitions during this period without undue stress. Large, stronger species wintering outside tolerate such outings well. It is nevertheless understandable that softbill aviculturists primarily interested in breeding are reluctant to enter their birds in exhibitions – and as explained earlier, birds for breeding sometimes have minor imperfections which would lose them points in competitive classes.

Captive-bred softbills, particularly if hand-reared, are far more suitable for exhibition than those originating from the wild. Their high degree of tameness counts for a lot as they behave very steadily in their showcages. Captive-bred softbills invariably turn out to be cocks and although an abundance of cocks are useless to the breeder, they *do* form the majority of softbill entries at exhibitions. It is twice as difficult to get a pair of any birds into show condition as it is for just one – that is why exhibitors often buy singleton cocks. In many species which are physically sexable, the cocks are often spectacularly beautiful while hens are nondescript.

Softbills intended for showing should be confined to the showcage for the odd day over about six weeks prior to the event. The cage should be roughly decorated also to correspond to the intended exhibit. Such training will ensure that the bird does not panic on the actual day, as he will have become used to the showcage beforehand. It need not take place prior to subsequent exhibitions. Try not to catch the bird to avoid disturbing the plumage. Ideally it should be tempted into the showcage by transferring food into it. Maintaining perfect condition before the show involves regular bathing – something the majority of softbills do anyway – but for those unwilling to bathe naturally, a fine daily spray with warm water from a pot-plant hand sprayer will help. Apart from offering titbits by hand to increase tameness, there is little else the exhibitor can do. An unexpected moult, the loss of or damage to feathers, and similar problems sometimes occur just before an exhibition. Then the exhibitor must decide whether it is still worthwhile entering the bird. Long-tailed softbills are understandably the most accident-prone in this respect. Do not overshow any bird. Five one-day shows, or three longer shows per season, should be the maximum.

Showcages

The wide variety of softbill shapes and sizes makes the standardization of showcages impossible. There is, however, a generally accepted *style* of softbill showcages, it being recognized that the size, fittings and interior furnishings will differ greatly. Figure 6 shows the style, but each dimension is variable. Super-active hummingbirds require a very large cage relative to their size. Chats, redstarts and other ground softbills need plenty of floor space though not so much height. Long-tailed species naturally require quite high showcages.

Only in painting can standardization be said to exist. Showcages are universally gloss black outside and gloss white inside. The cage fronts (bars) should be black as this enables easier viewing of the exhibit, but white ones are sometimes seen and these should not bring penalization. Great care must be taken of showcages, for if two identically perfect exhibits are competing for top honours and there is nothing to choose between them, the condition of the showcage may

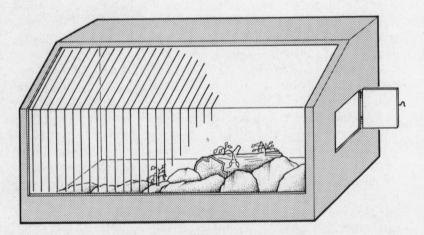

Figure 6 *Showcage of conventional softbill style*

be the deciding factor. Clean, well-painted ones are obviously more pleasing than chipped and grubby showcages.

Decorating showcages

Undoubtedly small and non-destructive softbills, together with all terrestrial species, look far more attractive in a sensibly decorated showcage – and good decoration impresses the average judge. However, all materials used should be *natural* and placed as realistically as possible. One sees – though fortunately not often – awful monstrosities composed largely of imitation things such as plastic flowers.

All items of decoration may be collected from woodland, and consist of various mosses, semi-rotted boughs from silver birches or other attractive trees, pieces of bark, wild ferns and pebbles. Removing the cage front, decoration of the showcage – landscaping in miniature – should take place the day before the show and kept in a cool place overnight to keep the plant life fresh. There is no limit or restriction to decoration but try to decorate according to the bird's natural habitat and don't overdo any decoration.

For destructive softbills and all the large species – jays, mynahs, magpies, fruit pigeons, blue rollers – decoration is impossible as they will quickly ruin it. Such birds are exhibited in cages containing only a couple of perches and thick white paper floor covering. Surplus wallpaper, pattern face down, is excellent floor covering material for showcages.

To and from the show

Rail delays have been responsible for some terrible problems where distant aviculturists have despatched birds to shows by train. It is therefore preferable for entries to be personally delivered and collected. Car transport is obviously best as this allows safe and adequately warm delivery to the building itself. Showcages *must* be covered with thick polythene, or contained within a wooden carrying case when transporting to and from shows, to avoid the birds becoming chilled. Remember it will be winter, and almost certainly very cold. A check-in procedure applies at all exhibitions, involving stewards recording that exhibits have been received. Exhibitors will have previously received by post a small cage label. This is filled in with class and entry number and stuck to the wooden rail immediately below the cage front. Judging takes place during the morning – the public being admitted in the afternoon – and winning entries will have their cages adorned with special labels and rosettes. Exhibitors collect their birds during the early evening when the public have left, going through the check-*out* procedure, which is like the check-in one. These procedures are for security and are very important.

Temperature changes

Cold halls are obviously damaging to birds which have been used to warmth, and show organizers often fail to recognize their responsibilities in this direction. There are power points in halls let out for functions and electric heaters can be hired; though show organizers and perhaps stewards and others connected with the event may be willing to bring a heater from their homes for a few hours. Such an arrangement would make a welcome improvement and perhaps encourage reluctant exhibitors to enter. The heaters need only be directed towards the foreign birds – warmth not being required by budgerigars, canaries and British birds which constitute the other sections of bird exhibitions. Further, they need only be switched on until the public are admitted, as the heat generated by them will soon raise the hall temperature. Known delicate specimens (invariably within the foreign softbill classes) would benefit enormously by having polythene draped over their cages, allowing air to enter, of course, again just until the hall fills with people.

The problem can then arise that the birds have been subjected to a higher temperature than necessary for several hours, so have the car heated for the journey home and, on arrival, leave the exhibits in a moderately warmed room, with a small night light, until morning. Rapid and drastic temperature changes are dangerous.

Contact with others

Occasionally an aviculturist will see a single exhibit at one of the major exhibitions, knowing that he has a singleton of the opposite sex. It is strongly recommended that he make contact with the exhibitor and that they agree that the one owning the most suitable accommodation should hold both birds and make a serious attempt to breed them. There is an understandable reluctance to do it, but aviculturists in that position should try to avoid the collector's weakness of not parting with a prized possession. One day it will die of old age, and if a sensible agreement can be made, both parties might have young to enjoy when the original birds have gone.

9

Ailments

Softbills do not have their own diseases – they are susceptible to all bird ailments – but there are certain problems associated more with softbills than other groups of birds. Since this book is about softbills, I shall deal with these but not describe the many and varied illnesses which affect all birds. Books exist on this subject exclusively. Perhaps the most important advice is: consult a vet with anything you do not recognize or feel competent to handle. Even for relatively simple illnesses, sometimes the necessary drug can only be obtained from a vet, or with one of his prescriptions. Softbill enthusiasts should find a local vet who has plenty of practical experience with birds (not all vets do because most of their work involves domestic pets, predominantly cats and dogs) and stay with him. It is cheaper to take an ailing bird to a vet rather than have him visit you, but the condition of the patient must decide this.

Bumblefoot

This condition results from softbills – more usually terrestrial species – having to perch on hard wood perches for long periods. It is rare indeed where natural twigs are provided, and renewed as they dry out and harden. Moss or peat should be used for floor covering where birds known to be susceptible are concerned. Softbills typically affected are pittas, redstarts, wagtails, chats, niltavas, ground thrushes and *all* waders. Bumblefoot, a form of arthritis, is where any or all of the leg joints are swollen. The swollen lumps are usually inflamed, and become hard if not treated quickly. This is one condition fairly easy to correct if treated early. Advanced cases are practically impossible to cure, and humane killing is the kindest thing to do since the joints become completely inoperative and the swellings are obviously painful.

If a softbill persistently holds one foot up, examine it for small inflamed swellings at the joints. These will be very small at first but treatment is necessary immediately. Transfer the bird to a cage with a floor covered with very slightly damp peat or moss. Remove all perches. The swellings will soon disappear, but if any of them have heads or minute cracks, penicillin ointment applied three times daily is of value. Antibiotics are generally useless although, under veterinary direction, could be effective in the unusual circumstance of bumble-foot being caused by the bird injuring itself and progressively weakening, with bumblefoot developing as a secondary infection.

Shock

Injury or any terrifying experience can cause shock. Shock is the violent disturbance of life's regular pattern, and if subjected to sufficient stress (frightening situations) shock is inevitable. A bird in shock cannot co-ordinate its movements and is a most distressing sight. It will try to fly but only be able to stagger around in circles. It will invariably have no control over its legs, and be unable to stand. Its vision will be out of balance – or its eyes closed – and it will only be semi-conscious. Any bird in shock should be placed in an open-topped box, lined with soft tissues. The top should be covered with muslin-like material, with extra air holes, and kept in a reasonably warm temperature. Avoid strong overhead lighting. Using a syringe, squeeze a little food (nectar is most practical at this stage) over the tongue into the crop, but do not force-feed or it could choke. Only handle for feeding attempts, otherwise leave strictly alone. In warm conditions, but not brilliantly lit, it will usually come out of shock after several hours. The bird will open its eyes and slowly recover general balance, but the ability to fly is slow in returning. Therefore keep it in the box for a day more, with a little food and water. Once completely conscious and standing properly, it should be transferred to a cage – still in the warm room – to enable the flight muscles to gently return to normality. Flying will be very wobbly at first and fairly subdued light is still necessary.

At several stages I have mentioned the need to avoid any foreseeable stressful situations since a build-up of stress can so easily develop into full shock. Careless handling, rapid movements, sudden noise, general commotion are all to be avoided. I have also explained that whilst night lights are important, at least in winter, they must not be too bright. The constant exposure to brilliant lighting will almost certainly lead to shock.

Aspergillosis

Aspergillosis is a fungus which occurs in damp and decaying vegetation. Inadequate ventilation in a hot and humid greenhouse/conservatory aviary will encourage the growth of moulds on discarded food particles, build-ups of droppings, and many other places; so increasing the risk that aspergillosis may develop. Airborne spores are inhaled by the birds and fungus grows on their lungs, making breathing difficult as it develops into a 'cheesey' mass affecting the whole respiratory system. Gasping is a typical symptom. Other birds in the same air space are at risk as they can inhale spores from the exhalations of those infected.

Again, stress will increase a bird's susceptibility to aspergillosis, the spores of which probably exist to some degree in all indoor softbill accommodation. The obvious prevention is to pay particular attention to hygiene so that mould-producing material is kept to the very minimum.

Something with almost identical symptoms is trichomoniasis. Similarly infectious, the fungus grows to the point where the respiratory systems become blocked. In advanced stages, it will corrode the tongue and is usually distinguishable from aspergillosis by the fact that it causes a nasty smell in the beak.

There are antibiotics capable of curing both these diseases if treated early, but only with a vet's prescription. At the first sign of any 'cheesey' substances in a softbill's mouth or on the tongue, veterinary advice is urgently recommended; and keep the suspect bird away from others.

Botulism

This is a form of food poisoning which can also affect humans. In England there was a big scare recently when a type of botulism was found in some tinned salmon and unexpected fatalities occurred among the elderly people who had eaten it. Botulism with softbills is the form associated with uncleaned maggots. It is caused by toxins produced from gut bacteria within the maggots – presumably derived from the decomposing meat on which maggots are commercially grown. It is to avoid this awful poisoning that maggots *must* be thoroughly cleaned in bran, as described earlier, before using them as softbill food. Before the bran treatment, most maggots are just as impure externally as they are in the gut, so cleaning really is vital.

In birds, the symptom for botulism is mainly paralysis – the legs hanging parallel with the wings and the bird being unable to move except flop along on its belly. If botulism were known to exist before this obvious symptom was seen, it may be more likely to respond to treatment, but invariably paralysis affecting all the nervous system, allied to a weakened condition, make the chances of survival slim. It has been claimed that orally syringing Epsom Salts diluted with warm water will force the bird to excrete the impurities along with everything else, and then it will be all right. It is hard to believe that this would work, however, as surely doctors would have successfully applied it to the unfortunate human patients mentioned earlier.

Pneumonia

Simple chills, especially if coupled to a sudden deterioration in weather conditions, can easily develop into pneumonia. This should always be suspected if a softbill stops eating, becomes inactive and sleeps for long periods on *both* feet with puffed-up plumage. Immediate removal to a hospital cage or somewhere with a temperature of 26 to 30°C, is essential. Warmth alone often provides a cure – the temperature *gradually* being reduced a degree or so daily when the patient is feeding normally and is active again – but various medicines are available which help.

Rapid temperature changes are mainly to blame for pneumonia, but it is much more commonly the cause of death in unfeathered chicks who, for one reason or another, become chilled in the nest. It is for this reason that breeding outside the summer months should not be encouraged.

Conjunctivitis

Bacteria or some other foreign body in the eye will cause this condition. It is invariably the result of a bird wiping its face on contaminated perching, although there are of course numerous other ways of getting impurities into the eye. The effect is that the eye will water and become inflamed around its edge. In obvious discomfort, the bird frequently opens and closes the infected eye, closing it completely if nothing is done. Further negligence will result in the eye sealing, with a puss-like substance visible and increasing inflammation. As with all other things, it can usually be cured if treated early. To delay makes treatment much more complicated and the necessary handling can induce stress and secondary conditions.

Treatment simply consists of bathing the eye with *warm* water containing a pinch of salt. When dry, one of the several veterinary opthalmic ointments are applied three times daily until the eye seems back to normal. This is squeezed *along* the eye and allowed to drop on to it. Contact with the warm eye melts the ointment and allows it to work. Do not touch the eye with the tube nozzle and try not to get surplus ointment on the face surrounding the eye, as it seems to remove the tiny face feathers. Finally, do not rub the ointment into the eye. Just let the little sausage of it fall on to the eye and melt.

A selection of softbilled birds

In this chapter, a selection of softbills are described, covering both common and rare specimens from each of the groupings (omnivorous, frugivorous, etc.) which I have found to be successful captive subjects once established and acclimatized. The choice has not been easy – there are countless species omitted due to the limited number of pages available – but I have given priority to covering at least one example from many of the most popular families. Those chosen are in no special order but cover a broad cross-section of the enormous softbill population from tiny honeycreepers to giant hornbills.

Rollers

Indian blue roller (*Coracias benghalensis*)
Grouping: insectivore

At the approach of spring, this common Indian bird becomes greatly excited, flying high, then plunging down, wings beating fast and creating more noise than usual with its loud, raucous cries. So it is this curious display which is responsible for the bird's name – nothing to do with its voice as many people, influenced no doubt by the roller canary, often think. The rolling flight is only obvious in the spring – the bird living a fairly sedentary life at other times. It prefers a high, thin perch on which it will sit motionless for long periods. It is always alert, no matter how relaxed it may look, for immediately an insect is seen, it will dart off and catch it with astonishing speed. It can hawk flying insects though much prefers to study the ground for such things as crickets and very small reptiles. Each time something is caught, the roller returns to his lofty position to eat it and resume watch.

This indication of its natural feeding technique will underline the need for crickets and/or locusts in the captive diet, together with as wide a variety of other insects as possible. Once a roller has settled down, he will quickly delight in catching mealworms when tossed, and such a daily ritual will provide useful exercise for the bird as he has to fly in varying directions and heights. Baby mice, with little or no fur, are also of tremendous value in the diet of any captive roller.

The rolling displays of springtime can only be possible in captivity if a very big aviary is available – and then the vivid light blues and dark blues present in wings and tail will be seen at their very best. The roller has very small feet and the natural desire for thin, high perches has already been mentioned.

Several rollers may be kept in a large aviary with minimal bickering *if all introduced together* and it is only in this way that a pair may emerge since the sexes are alike; yet in spite of their heavy build and harsh voice, they are not dangerous to smaller birds. They spend most of their time at the very top of the aviary, sunning themselves when there is any sun, and keeping their very large black eyes open for insects, just as they would do in their homeland – typically on power wires. Otherwise known as a blue jay although not at all related to proper jays, the Indian blue roller is well distributed throughout India, extending to Burma and Thailand, as well as Sri Lanka where, with racial differences, it is *C. b. indica*. There are several other races – all basically similar – but which are not available to aviculture so much.

Other rollers occasionally figuring in collections include the very beautiful **Lilac-breasted** (*Coracias cuadata*) from South Africa, which is much like the Indian blue but with a deeply forked tail which adds some 5 cms to its length; and the **South-East Asian dollar birds** (*Eurystomus orientalis*). I remember once hand-rearing some baby dollar birds which possessed the most harsh, grating cries imaginable. Typical of all rollers, dollar birds have very small and weak feet, but highly developed wings enabling not only the hawking of flying insects, but breathtaking aerial displays. Dollar birds can rise and fall in flight even more spectacularly than other rollers though, garbed mainly in deep blue, they are not so pretty. Their wide, coral-red beaks can open enough to accommodate surprisingly large insects, but their name derives from the silvery discs on the chests of adults, which obviously reminded whoever christened them of silver dollars.

Yuhinas

Black-chinned yuhina (*Yuhina nigrimenta*)
Grouping: insect-biased omnivore

Throughout South-East Asia are the nine-strong family of small crested softbills known in aviculture by their latin name – yuhinas. They all belong to the large and ill-assorted babbler group, sharing typical characteristics of sociability, continual chattering and rapid, fairly acrobatic movement. Though none are brightly coloured, they have enormous charm and this, allied to their lack of aggression in mixed collections, make them established favourites among all enthusiasts.

Of all yuhinas, it is only the black-chinned which is usually available; originating invariably from Northern India, where flocks frequent widespread areas of secondary forest growth. They are not always easy to see, though their presence is betrayed by their characteristic chatter.

Though requiring careful handling during quarantine, these are easy subjects once established and will live harmoniously with other small babblers, honeycreepers, zosterops and tanagers to name but a few. Being sexually alike, it is difficult to select a pair, though by studying the behaviour of several, a pair can usually be found. When given a well-planted aviary (preferably to themselves) a pair of yuhinas will often breed, always building, in my experience, their own nest within fairly thick bushes. A breeding pair can of course be returned to a communal aviary after the breeding season if desired. Yuhinas are one of the half-hardy species, requiring some protection during the winter.

All that has been said of the above applies equally well to the occasionally available **Yellow-naped yuhina** (*Yuhina flavicollis*) which, through common usage, is more generally known as yellow-naped ixulus. At some 10 cms long it is longer than *Y. nigrimenta* by about 2 cms, and is noticeably plumper. Wintertime accommodation, which will invariably be smaller than the summer aviary, should nevertheless be as generous as possible since the ixulus is very prone to putting on unwanted weight.

From Sikiang province in China, and North-East Burma, comes the much larger **White-collared yuhina** (*Yuhina diademata*) which is one of the creatures discovered by the legendary Père David. Both sexes are greyish brown, darker above than below, with yellow eyes and legs. The distinctive white part which provides its common name occupies the area behind each eye, covering the nape of the neck where it broadens. This exceedingly appealing bird has been found at low altitudes around 500 metres, but more usually inhabits higher altitudes ranging from 1500 to 2500 metres.

Another yuhina hardly known in captivity is the striking **Rufous-vented yuhina** (*Yuhina occipitalis*) which lives in the typical flocks at similar heights in the Himalayas of Sikkim, Nepal and Bhutan as well as the same range as the white-collared. Only a centimetre longer than the well-known black-chinned, this yuhina is basically russet brown above, more fawn below, head and front half of crest grey, while the back half down to the shoulders is bright rufous.

Hornbills

Red-billed hornbill (*Tokus erythrorhynchus rufirostris*)
Grouping: omnivore

Hornbills, because of their size, are mainly kept by zoos and bird gardens, but in the red-billed is the perfect member of this family for private aviculturists who admire the birds but may not possess enormous aviaries. This pretty hornbill is only some 46 cms in total length and has a more docile nature than its larger relatives, enabling other large softbills to be kept in the same aviary.

Although an omnivore, extra meat is important. Dead day-old chicks, dead mice, strips of raw meat, all figure in the diet of a hornbill; small species such as this appreciate locusts as well. In the wild, the red-billed eats a lot of insects from the dry ground of the South African bush. Living in pairs or small flocks, they will fly in the heavy, laborious way of all hornbills, quite long distances to feast upon the plentiful livefood displaced by bush fires. Two similar subspecies exist, their latin names reflecting the archaic tribal-land names of the Southern African lands in which they are localized: *T. e. ngamiensis* in which the bill is slightly longer, and *T. e. damarensis* in which it is still longer. All, however, are very similar.

The remarkable nesting procedure of hornbills, whereby the hen is literally walled-up inside her nesting chamber for the duration of incubation, applies to these small species just the same. When a hole in a tree (usually very high up) has been selected, the hornbills begin plastering mud, droppings and rotted leaf material all around its edge. When just as small as it can be before admission is impossible, the hen goes in and makes the base of the nesting chamber to her liking, while the cock continues plastering the entrance hole, imprisoning her inside, and leaving only a tiny slot. Through this he feeds his mate for the whole nesting period, which is around six weeks for species like the little red-billed and double that for the giants of the family. The red-billed are unusual in that they will sometimes take a few leaves into the disused woodpecker hole they so often adapt as their own nest. Most hornbills do not use nesting material as such. Anything from one to six fairly round white eggs can be laid, with three to four forming the more average clutch. Allowing twenty-eight to thirty days to hatch (for red-billed) and around forty for large hornbills, the hen remains imprisoned half as long again while the chicks are developing, behind the now rock-hard plastered entrance.

When the chicks are about half grown, the use for the hornbill's strong beak is shown, for the hen will hammer at the edges of the feeding slot, enlarging it sufficiently for her to pass through. Invariably the chicks will replaster the gap with their own faeces when she has gone, to re-secure the nesting chamber in case of predators, leaving again just a feeding slot. The reason for the hen's departure at this stage is that she has to assist the cock in bringing food to the nest. He finds it difficult to provide enough food for the entire family as the chicks develop and want ever-increasing amounts.

In common with their larger relatives, the red-billed usually form a life-long pair bond, and will accept a barrel raised on stilts with an entrance hole near the top. Although captive breeding is not common, they will live many years without falling ill if plenty of meat is included in the diet and, when acclimatized, will winter outdoors quite safely.

Another fairly small hornbill, but this time from South-East Asia, is the appealing **Southern pied** (*Anthracoceros convexus*) which, though not common, has been available several times during the last few years. My experience with them has been limited to two small groups of babies received when almost independent and so requiring hand feeding for some days. They had of course been taken from the nest and hand-reared prior to shipping and were very humanized. It is said that they are frequently kept as pets in Malaya.

Unlike the African hornbills, these have a casque above their beaks – a typical feature of Asiatic hornbills, the most spectacular of which is the **Rhinoceros hornbill** (*Buceros rhinoceros*) whose casque points upward from the beak, resembling a rhino's horn. There is much uncertainty about the purpose of these casques, which weigh little as they are cellular in structure, but one logical theory is that they act as shock-absorbers when the birds are hammering trees or demolishing their plastering. Large hornbills certainly have very strong bills and sometimes become very destructive, so that explanation sounds reasonable.

Flycatchers

Verditer flycatcher (*Muscicapa thalassina*)
Grouping: insectivore

Of the 328 species of flycatcher which inhabit the world, this is by far the most well known among aviculturists. Its long popularity owes much to the fact that it is easy to establish in comparison to most others. The illustration is of a male – the females are duller blue and small white spots pepper the throat when adult. The bill is very wide at its base, which is surrounded with hairs.

Though half-hardy, pairs will breed in planted aviaries during the summer, building their own cup-like nests in suitable bushes but they are remarkably unsettled when breeding and rush off the nest in fright at the sight of even those they know. This behaviour is surprising since, when not breeding, they are among the boldest of birds. It could be that this is why breedings are rare, since there must be a reasonable number of verditer pairs in aviculture.

Single males make good show birds, their bold upright stance never failing to impress; and their beautiful verditer blue plumage rendering them very conspicuous.

The verditer has an enormous range, from India to South China and even occurs on the islands of Borneo and Sumatra. Throughout India, the typical race is an adaptable creature, seeming to be equally happy in the jungle and in parks and gardens. It is not shy and is frequently seen catching flying insects in the typical flycatcher manner. It is a dedicated bather, and this point is of major importance since in captivity many die through bathing with excessive zeal. They emerge from the water thoroughly water-logged and seem reluctant to shake themselves and preen. In standing like that they inevitably become chilled and succumb. This behaviour is odd and is why they are not recommended for tropical houses where the pools are usually quite deep. A depth of only about 2 cms should be the maximum water for this species.

There are many other flycatchers and related species available from the South-East Asian region generally and with the exception of only one or two, they take to substitute diets and become very desirable subjects, though perhaps the verditer is traditionally the best loved.

The little flycatchers from Africa known as wattle eyes do not adapt so well and seem prone to vitamin deficiencies but are nevertheless worthy of a place in any thoroughly professional collection, where their demands may be understood and met. The illustration is of the East African **Black-throated wattle eye** (*Platysteira peltata*) female. A lot has still to be learned of their requirements, and a valuable study to ascertain the best captive environment is badly needed. Coming as they do from hot and fairly dry conditions, it seems certain that the tropical house kind of environment which one would assume they like could be most unsuitable. It would be interesting to see if a *dry* atmosphere would suit them better – perhaps a conventional tropical house building but with sand, not peat flooring, a very small pool, thorny bush vegetation, water-conserving plants instead of water-loving ones. In zoos, many reptile exhibits are of this type. However, since wattle eyes are rarely available there seems little opportunity for such useful experiments to be carried out.

Euphonias

Thick-billed euphonia (*Euphonia laniirostris*)
Grouping: fruit-biased omnivore

From Mexico, through all the Central American countries and down to about halfway through the South American continent, come the twenty-four small tanagers known as euphonias. They are a common sight in areas where fruit is cultivated and also spend much time around jungle edges seeking the various forms of berry which comprise their major diet. Pairs may separate from the normal flock when breeding but euphonias are generally gregarious by nature, as are the vast majority of tanagers.

Euphonias are plumpish birds some 10 cms long, mostly very similar to each other, and when several have arrived in mixed batches it has proved extremely difficult to identify them with total accuracy. The illustration is of a male, whose plumage is typical of most – all under parts and crown being yellow, while upper parts including tail, are glossy blue-black. Two white spots are on the tail if viewed from above, so these do not show in the illustration. A few regularly imported euphonias have a little blue on the throat. Females are mainly dull olive with a yellowish green belly, thus enabling sexing at a glance. It must be mentioned, however, that immatures of both sex resemble the female. I have watched euphonias in the wild and have always found difficulty in locating females since their colour blends perfectly with foliage. Patient watching is always rewarded, however, by keeping an eye on the more obvious males because the females are always close by.

Aviculturally, they have many good points – strong constitutions not normally prone to disorders, hardiness since with sensible protection they will winter outdoors, ease of sexing, willingness to breed and lack of aggression among other similar sized softbills. In addition, either a pair or a single male are capable of major wins at exhibitions.

Whereas the typical (*Tangara*) tanagers accept a small cup-shaped nesting basket, or build their own of that style, euphonias make fairly distinctive domed nests. Having laid their eggs, the females do almost all the thirteen to fourteen days of incubating unaided, though males are excellent parents and assist in feeding the young which, surprisingly, is done by regurgitation.

Chlorophonias

Blue-naped chlorophonia (*Chlorophonia cyanea*)
Grouping: fruit-biased omnivore

Rarer and much more difficult to maintain are the four chlorophonias. In this family, females are similarly marked to their mates but less vividly, so sexing is fairly simple. They are of course related to the euphonias – sharing the same build and habits – though have a far more restricted range. They are high altitude birds, found predominantly in the Colombian Andes, though the more numerous blue-naped extends to Guyana, Ecuador, Peru and other neighbouring countries. The illustration is of a male blue-naped, in which two races are recognized – *C. c. psittacina*, and *C. c. longipennis* – the latter is the one illustrated. The only chlorophonia to have pushed into Central America is the blue-crowned (*C. occipitalis*) which seems to have adapted to lowland conditions more successfully than others are capable of doing.

It is this point, combined with the fact that they are not plentiful anyway, that makes them difficult to establish in Europe. They are invariably kept in excessive heat and the few that are in aviculture would be better kept outdoors for all but the winter. As can be seen, the family are extremely beautiful and are about the same size as euphonias; but unlike euphonias they are not good beginner's subjects.

Barbets

Fire-headed barbet (*Capito bourcierii*)
Grouping: fruit-biased omnivore

The barbets are a large and varying family, represented in three continents – Africa, Asia and South America. Allowing for the differences in size, shape of beak, colouration etc., they all share similar habits. They are strictly arboriel forest dwellers with heavy bodies, large heads and powerful beaks, tufts fringing the nostrils, short and stubby wings and whose favourite occupation is uttering monotonous calls for long periods! Most live largely on fruit and insects, though some are almost entirely insectivorous. These need not concern us as they are hardly ever obtainable and unlikely to be so for the foreseeable future. The African tinker birds are the most well known of such birds.

Since the wide variety of barbets exported for aviculture are all fruit eaters, they are an easy group to manage and have always been popular. It must be emphasized however that fruit alone is not an adequate captive diet (see Feeding chapter). Barbets are, in spite of their robust appearance, only half hardy so must have wintertime protection. They are related to woodpeckers, with whom they share similar nesting habits, though they excavate their nesting chambers by digging the wood rather than hammering it. In captivity all barbets derive much pleasure from this form of woodwork, so semi-rotted pieces of tree trunks are most valuable items for their aviaries. I have always favoured silver birch trees for this purpose since they are soft, and partly rotted lengths can always be collected from woodlands.

It is possible that a pair would excavate such a piece of wood and successfully breed, though in practice most barbet owners provide at least one nesting box for their pairs, sometimes surrounded with natural wood for demolition. Nesting boxes are important for all barbets because even if they do not breed in them, they invariably sleep in them. A small parakeet or lovebird-type nesting box is suitable, but where a known pair do exist every effort should be made to surround the box with soft natural wood to help stimulate an interest in breeding. Barbet eggs are white, two to four being the average clutch, and incubation lasts thirteen to fifteen days. The young develop slowly and usually remain in the nest longer than would be expected.

One reason why barbets are not bred more often in captivity is because of the difficulty in sexing. Most are alike, but I have chosen the fire-headed because this is one of the few which can be sexed at a glance. Both male and female are illustrated indicating the sexual differences. The fire-headed barbet is South American, occurring in Venezuela, Ecuador, Colombia and Peru. At only about 12 cms, it is one of the smaller members of its family and, though typically aggressive, it can if necessary be housed with big tanagers and bulbuls, for example. On no account should it (or any other barbet) be kept with smaller birds.

The aptly-named **Gaudy barbet** (*Megalaima mystacophanos*) is one of the more impressive Asiatic barbets. It is larger than the former species, at some 16 cms, and is a worthwhile addition to any softbill collection. It is a bird of the hot lowlands, living in forest habitats mainly in Malaya and Thailand, together with Sumatra and Borneo. This and other *Megalaima* barbets are much addicted to wood digging, as their strong black beaks indicate, and benefit from a rather higher amount of animal protein than the South American ones. Their natural habitat also gives a clue to their need for indoor housing as soon as winter approaches.

Birds of paradise

Red-plumed bird of paradise (*Paradisaea apoda raggiana*)
Grouping: fruit-biased omnivore

Shrouded in mystery and the subjects of legend, these birds have aroused man's imagination since their discovery over 400 years ago. In 1522 Magellan took two skins from a local island ruler in the Moluccas who wished them be presented to the Spanish king. The Spaniards considered them so beautiful that the birds must have come from paradise and christened them accordingly. That was the first time any of these birds had been seen in Europe and the name has remained ever since.

Subsequently, of course, other species were discovered since a large trade had developed in buying the birds' skins from local tribesmen and taking them to European fashion centres where they were used to adorn ladies' millinery creations. By the late 1800s an astonishing 50,000 skins were annually going to the millinery markets, where excited ornithologists sorted them for new species. This appalling slaughter must have pushed many to near extinction, and today we can only hypothesize on how common they once were. It is generally considered that there are forty-three different birds of paradise living in New Guinea and its satellite islands. Many live in the highlands and remain mysterious creatures about which relatively little is known; others are more accessible and of these, three have come into aviculture during recent years, originating from Indonesian-governed islands. These are little king (*Cicinnurus regius*), Wilson's (*Diphyllodes republica*) and the illustrated red-plumed. Although he has moulted his spectactular red plumes which extend some 36 cms from the flanks, the picture shows a good example of what everybody expects a bird of paradise to look like. The *Paradisaea* genus comprises six similar examples of which the red-plumed is perhaps the most common. The breast colouration distinguishes one from another – ranging from the grey-breasted to orange.

The accumulated avicultural experience with birds of paradise is limited and, in the main, unsatisfactory. As with the chlorophonia discussed earlier, a regular fault has been housing them in a hot, closed atmosphere whereas many species live at high altitudes in the wild. Descended as they have from ancient crows, they would seem to be easily managed subjects, and indeed a wide diet as described for the fruit-biased omnivores has proved acceptable for the few captive specimens which have graced aviculture to date.

From one genus to another, there is little doubt that birds of paradise are aptly named and provide the most incredible examples of avian beauty imaginable. It is sad that faded museum skins and inaccurate paintings are all that most people will see of such fantastic birds.

Bulbuls

Red-whiskered bulbul (*Pycnonotus jocosus*)
Grouping: fruit-biased omnivore

Moving from birds of paradise to bulbuls is literally looking at both extremes of the avicultural spectrum since the latter are super-abundant, highly adaptable, simple to keep and cheap to buy. This is not to decry them at all – quite the contrary. Few birds can have made such a contribution to softbill aviculture, for within the family are less common species to interest the experienced, and the regularly available ones typified by the red-whiskered which are perfect beginner's birds. Whether common or less so, all bulbuls are very undemanding subjects which, following their natural omnivorous ways, will eat virtually anything they are offered in captivity. They are generally hardy enough to remain outdoors throughout the year, though understandably there are less strong exceptions to this rule. All those normally available are hardy, however.

Bulbuls have enormous ranges throughout Asia and Africa. Many are lowland birds but some extend to surprising altitudes in excess of 3000 metres above sea level. They are highly gregarious, very active, have small crests which in some species are not very obvious, vary in length from about 12 to 20 cms and generally possess pleasing songs. Sexes are alike, even juveniles resembling their parents though they can usually be distinguished by vestiges of their fleshy gapes still showing at the sides of the beak for many months.

Most species coming into aviculture arrive from various parts of Indo-China; the equally common African species only arriving at odd intervals because many African exporters concentrate on the more lucrative parrots and reptiles.

The red-whiskered bulbul has always been a common bird in India where there are five races, three having white tips to the tail and two lacking these markings. The races are fairly localized, a simplified distinction being that the northern races are basically lowland dwellers, while the southern ones frequent higher altitudes. They shun jungle areas in favour of villages, gardens and cultivated land generally, showing no fear of man. They nest in bushes, rarely more than 2 metres from the ground, building a cup-shaped nest, rather like a small blackbird's and lined with fine grasses, while dried leaves are woven into the base. From this it will be seen that their captive breeding requirements present few problems.

Slightly larger, at some 16 cms instead of 14, the two other very common bulbuls generally available are Red-vented (*Molpastes cafer*) and White-cheeked (*M. leucogenys*), the latter having a prominent forward-pointing crest.

Forest bee-eaters

Red-bearded bee-eater (*Nyctyornis amictus*)
Blue-bearded bee-eater (*Nyctyornis athertoni*)
Grouping: insectivore

These two bee-eaters not only look different to the other twenty-two species which inhabit the Old World but occupy totally different habitat. They could be called forest bee-eaters for they live in thick jungle and are fairly sedentary except when actually catching some flying insect or other. They will also swoop to the ground to grasp any passing insect, rather than restricting themselves to hawking on the wing. Another aspect of their behaviour unique among bee-eaters is that, save at breeding times, they are solitary birds.

Rare birds from Indo-China, the red-bearded is approximately 25 cms in total length and females are not so brilliant at the crown; while the blue-bearded is 2 cms more and sexually similar. Although very beautiful, they have harsh voices and their heavy build combined with sluggish behaviour has reduced their following to just a dedicated few. I count myself among the few for I have kept both species for lengthy periods and thoroughly enjoyed it. To establish such birds is difficult, but if achieved is most rewarding as they develop great friendliness. Unfortunately, mine cast large quantities of pellets. These were ejected with force and unfortunately stained the wall and any other surface they landed on! Having not seen either on the showbench, I entered a pair of blue-bearded at a recent national exhibition to ascertain their reaction. Although fairly tame beforehand, the experience seemed to disturb (not frighten) them at first, though after the first night there they resumed feeding in their raucous way and appeared to take the change of environment in their stride.

The bearded bee-eaters have heavier beaks than other species, which they use to good advantage with large insects, holding them tightly and pounding them on the perch until broken or sufficiently reshaped to swallow. Their feet are small and weak, however, a characteristic of all hawking species; but this is counteracted by strong and powerful wings, without which their feeding method would be impossible.

Open country bee-eaters

Carmine bee-eater (*Merops nubicus*)
European bee-eater (*Merops apiaster*)
Grouping: insectivore

Most typical bee-eaters are contained in the *Merops* genera and possess the features associated with bee-eaters by most people: a slim stream-lined body, long slightly curved beaks, superb fast flight, and leading a highly gregarious life. They live in large groups, in sunny, open country and as their name implies, consume about half of their food in the form of wild bees and wasps of various kinds. Flies and other winged insects complete the diet, all being caught in flight.

The carmine is very abundant in East Africa where it gives up its arboreal life at breeding times to excavate a deep nesting tunnel in exposed vertical earth banks. No nesting material is taken to the actual chamber at the end of the tunnel and the two to eight eggs require approximately twenty-two days to incubate. Almost twenty-eight days later the young emerge, covered in pin-feathers.

In captivity the lovely red in the carmine's plumage is prone to fading unless some colour food is injected into their livefood through each moult; but though this is the only safe way of getting the colour food into them, it cannot be administered in large enough amounts to stop fading altogether. It cannot be introduced in drinking water since bee-eaters are thought not to drink, adequate moisture being obtained from the insects they eat.

The European bee-eater occurs in Southern Europe, parts of Asia and Africa. It is only 20 cms in total length, against some 24 for the carmine, and the plumage does not fade since it contains no red.

Merops and related bee-eaters are notoriously difficult to establish due to their natural hawking method of feeding, but those that do successfully transfer to a substitute diet (including many flies, meal-worms and small crickets which they catch when tossed in the air) usually thrive for many years in normal tropical house environments.

Toucans

Toco toucan (*Ramphastos toco*)
Grouping: fruit-biased omnivore

The four groups of toucans total some thirty-seven species all restricted to tropical South and Central America, and forming one of the most distinctive families. They all socialize among their kind, roaming in noisy bands through the upper levels of forest in search of fruit and small unwary birds and reptiles. It is to enable a heavy-bodied bird to reach berries at the end of very thin twigs that nature has provided them with their enormous beaks, which are always brightly coloured. The beaks are of cellular structure and not at all as heavy as they look – otherwise toucans would be top-heavy. In virtually all cases, sexes are alike.

The toco (whose name is corrupted from the original Indian word for the toucans) is a member of the true, or typical toucans. The characteristic of these is that they are the largest of the four groups, mainly black with a concentration of colour around the face and beak. Tocos are found in Brazil, Paraguay and parts of Guyana and they are the largest toucan. They are sometimes taken from the nest and hand-reared, mainly so by the Amerindians of Guyana, but even adults adapt remarkably well to captive conditions and, as any zoo visitor will know, soon become favourites with everybody.

Another widely kept true toucan is the **Sulphur-breasted (***Ramphastos sulphuratus***)**, 4 cms shorter than the toco, at 44 cms, and ranging from Mexico (almost exclusively the southern part) to Venezuela. Aviculturally, these are perhaps the most desirable as their beaks are exceptionally attractive and they are the most hardy. Nevertheless, winter is usually too cold for them in these climes and so they should only be kept outdoors from, say, April to September.

The other three groups in the toucan family are the small green Toucanettes; Aracaris with black or grey-green upper parts and yellow-, red- and black-banded chests; Mountain-toucans, rarities with blue under parts, brown wings, and multi-coloured beaks. All thrive on the same treatment.

Broadbills

Lesser green broadbill (*Calyptomena viridis*)
Grouping: fruit-biased omnivore

This is the only member of the family to be seen in aviculture since it is commonest of the three broadbills which are omnivorous – all the other eleven species being hawking insectivores – and has a fairly wide distribution in the forests of South-East Asia.

The lesser green is typical of the family, being short and plump, with extremely wide beak, short legs but powerful feet equipped with uncommonly sharp claws. It is capable of rapid flight although when not feeding it spends much time draped sluggishly over its perch. It has very large eyes – perhaps to aid vision, since all broadbills inhabit deep jungle areas and cloud forests.

The illustration is of a male. Females do not have the black wing or ear markings, and are a paler green. Since they appear to take two years to reach maturity, some females turn out to be immature males eventually; but this slowness to mature would suggest a longish life span subject to all things being equal.

Ideal subjects for tropical houses or planted outdoor aviaries during the warm months, they are totally inoffensive and utter their intriguing call when excited. This is a very jungle-like sound rather similar to melodious bubbling and not at all unpleasant.

In the wild broadbills build very complex nests, consisting of deep pockets, woven from plant fibres; narrow at the tops, widening out as they go down, and then tapering to a point at the base. Inside this structure, the nesting chamber is situated at the widest part and lined with finer materials. The entrance hole is small and situated about two-thirds down its length, and the whole thing is suspended on a suitable branch overhanging water. If captive breeding is to take place, these notes will indicate the environment needed and that plenty of nesting material would be essential. Obviously birds of this type whose nesting is specialized would shun any artificial nesting baskets or boxes.

Most of the Asiatic species are basically bright green but with added colour around the face, and usually with fairly long tails. The lesser green only has a tiny tail, adding to its already squat appearance. Certain species are restricted to Borneo and Sumatra; while four are African. Though several are as plentiful in their respective ranges as the lesser green, they are not usually taken into aviculture as exporters consider the problems associated with their feeding are too great.

If any of the insectivorous broadbills were available, they would need the same painstaking meating-off process as used for bee-eaters.

Honeycreepers

Black-faced dacnis (*Dacnis lineata*)
Grouping: nectivore

A distant branch of the tanager family which have adapted to largely living on nectar are the rather jumbled thirty-strong family of small, exclusively Central and South American softbills collectively known as honeycreepers. Most well known by aviculturists are the so-called sugarbirds, (*Cyanerpes*), which are mainly blue in males and green in females, and which are characterized by long downward-curved beaks. The red-legged honeycreeper (*Cyanerpes cyaneus*) traditionally referred to as yellow-winged sugarbird in avicultural circles is the commonest. But the *Cyanerpes* are just one section of the honeycreeper family.

Another group – *Dacnis* – are much less known and the few that reach aviculture are usually lumped together with the similarly built *Iridophanes* and termed 'short-billed sugarbirds'. The illustrated Black-faced dacnis is a male – females are greyish brown above and indistinct olive below with off-white belly - and shows the short, pointed beak clearly, a feature common to the dacnis. Unlike the well-known *Cyanerpes*, these tend to be localized and live in far more inaccessible forest. They are also not so hardy or docile as their long-billed relatives but, as can be seen from the illustration, they are small exotics of extreme beauty.

The **Yellow-collared 'sugarbird'** (*Iridophanes pulcherrima*) at some 10 cms is slightly larger than the former but has the same habits and also lives in heavily forested areas. They too are easy to sex, the illustration being of a fine male. The short bills give an indication that these birds favour a high proportion of insect life. Certainly they do need more than the more nectivorous *Cyanerpes* but not greatly so. Indeed, if they arrive healthy this whole family are fairly easy to quarantine and get established though being relatively scarce in aviculture, those that are available tend to be in the hands of only the most serious.

An odd little bird with only superficial likenesses, but which nevertheless is included in the honeycreeper family, is the exceedingly active **Banana quit** (*Coereba flaveola*), the six races of which cover a huge range. Virtually every Central and South American country has them, together with may of the Caribbean islands. It is widespread in all cultivated areas and is a regular visitor to gardens. Lacking shyness and preferring to live near humans contributes much to its remarkable success and, of course, being easy to fix nets in such localities means that in countries where export is permitted, this is one of the commonest birds exported. Indications are that most are sent to America for in England we only receive a few occasionally now, whereas until about 1972 they were abundant.

In aviculture they are perhaps the easiest of all honeycreepers to manage, which one would expect from such an adaptable and widespread bird, and tolerate lower temperatures than all other species.

Nevertheless some heat is required for the coldest months. In mixed softbill collections, they tend to become what zebra finches are to the hardbill enthusiast. They have the annoying habit of poking about in other nests, giving the impression of wishing to use it themselves but then, when the original occupants have been evicted, they either lose interest in it themselves or pull it apart. This, allied to their surprisingly quarrelsome natures, mean that they are not recommended for communal aviaries. On their own, or with bigger birds, they are no trouble and indeed their constant activity and friendliness towards their owner make them desirable subjects.

Worthy of mention are the specialized feeders **Flower-piercers** (*Diglossas*) which with **Conebills** (*Conirostrum species*) complete the greatly varied honeycreeper family. Flower-piercers have unique beaks where the upper mandible is hooked over the lower at its tip. Alighting on flowers with tubular corollas, the shaped upper mandible holds them still while the lower mandible pierces the corollas. Through the small hole the flower-piercers then sip the nectar. Before moving on, their tongues flick around the flowers for small insects as well. Masked flower-piercers (*Diglossa cyanea*) and to a lesser extent black flower-piercers (D. carbonaria) were available until the early 1970s but would be rarities on the avicultural scene nowadays. They are highland birds and therefore somewhat difficult to locate. From those I handled in the past, I consider them to be good avicultural subjects, living very largely on nectar and livefood, with little liking for fruit, but leading a fairly solitary existence and intolerant of other similar sized companions or smaller.

Spiderhunters

Spectacled spiderhunter (*Arachnothera flavigaster*)
Grouping: nectivore

Restricted to fairly localized ranges in South-East Asia, the very distinctive small family of spiderhunters are a branch of the sunbirds which are not blessed with iridescent plumage but are equally desirable to the softbill enthusiast. All spiderhunters are various shades of green, with yellow present in facial markings. The streak-breasted has strong black streaking down its breast but others are more plain. Their beaks are very long and down-curved, their legs and feet are strong while the claws are very sharp indeed. They are chattery birds, calling to each other regularly but, in captivity at least, groups usually squabble so I separate them into pairs when I have them. Spiderhunters vary in length from some 10 cms to 14 and are strong fliers.

The illustration shows the upright and typically alert stance of the family and their attractive structure. In captivity they all exhibit the same habits and, after settling into a new environment, usually become very tame. This is unexpected as they are shy and retiring in the wild, yet it is no exaggeration to say that with a little patience, spiderhunters will become finger tame inside a month.

They do very well in aviaries and although I know of a case where they wintered out, it is safer to treat spiderhunters as only half hardy. Compared to true sunbirds, they are more robust, sampling all kinds of foods and taking a deep interest in all that goes on around them. Sexing is difficult and, like broadbills, they build a very special nest. It is a very small woven cup-shaped nest but literally sewn to the underside of a broad leaf. Banana trees are favoured since their leaves are ideal for the purpose. The stitching is cast off with a knot at regular intervals, the knots being visible from above the leaf, which forms the nest roof. All duties involved in nest building and raising the family (usually just two babies) are shared by both parents.

Kingfishers

Stork-billed kingfishers (*Pelargopsis capensis*)
Grouping: carnivore

Apart from the polar areas of the world, kingfishers occur in all continents though the majority are Asiatic. It is important to distinguish between the two subfamilies since only species from one are suitable for aviculture. The well-known European or common kingfisher *Alcedo atthis* is typical of the *Alcedininae* kingfishers which have thin, sharp beaks and actually catch fish, which forms their diet. These are the types which have so far proved almost impossible to maintain in captivity as they will not eat fish unless it is alive and caught by themselves. Enclosing a large stretch of water well stocked with minnows, in a huge aviary, would probably be the only substituted environment they would accept; but this is costly and impractical to the extent that, as far as I know, *Alcedininae* have only once been exhibited by even a major zoo.

The other species are usually termed forest kingfishers and are of the subfamily *Daceloninae*. Apart from living in forested areas instead of open country, they are slower in their movements, usually larger in size and have flatish, wide beaks. But the vital difference aviculturally is that they do not rely on catching fish. Although they will certainly eat an unwary fish lingering near the water's edge if they can, the majority of their food consists of insects, amphibians, small reptiles, and rarely small rodents and birds. This makes catering for them in captivity quite feasible.

Our subject, the stork-billed, is found around forest streams in much of South-East Asia and is recorded on the Nicobar islands, Sundas, Celebes and many more. It is a substantial bird, some 27 cms in length, a good third of which is taken up by the enormous red beak – hence the name. It is one of the several species of forest kingfishers from that part of the world to have established well in captivity, though it is noisy. Anybody possessing tropical kingfishers should certainly allow them an aviary during summer but, with the notable exception of the Australian kookaburra (*Dacelo gigas*) they cannot withstand our winters without warmth.

Tits

Red-headed tit (*Aegithalos concinnus*)
Grouping: insectivore

The red-headed is probably the smallest of this familiar family, which is spread throughout Europe, Africa and Asia and is a favourite in aviculture. The acrobatic way in which parties of tits systematically work over trees and bushes in search of insects is a most absorbing sight and these movements are unhesitatingly demonstrated by the red-headed.

Although distributed from India to China it is not often available but, if sensibly packed it will travel well and establish without significant problems. Like all tits, it has the ability to hold an insect on the perch with its feet and eat it by pulling off pieces. In this way insects can be consumed which would be too big to swallow whole. Sexes are alike and they are delicate, though should have the benefit of fresh air during warm weather. Their minute build, attractive plumage, engaging ways and lack of aggression make them the ideal tit for any form of tropical house.

More often available and at cheaper prices are the **Green-backed tits** (*Parus monticolus*), which resemble in many ways the common English garden visitor, the great tit (*Parus major*), but are some 2 cms smaller. The green-backed is far more robust than the little red-headed and, with a small nesting box for sleeping in, is capable of wintering outdoors. It has a reputation for aggression but this has not been my experience and I would think the green-backed likely to breed if a pair could be selected since, like all tits, both sexes look alike.

Manakins

Red-capped manakin (*Pipra mentalis*)
Grouping: fruit-biased omnivore

Tropical Central and South America is the home of the fifty-odd species of manakins, all small and well-rounded birds which are generally sexable, live in small bands and are said to show little fear of man. Many are black bodied, with colour around the head as is indicated by the illustrated red-capped. This is a male but it does not show the bright yellow thighs clearly – this last feature providing its alternative common name, yellow-thighed manakin. His particular range is from Southern Mexico to Western Ecuador.

Manakins are forest birds, feeding on fruit (mainly small wild berries) and insects usually within the band from ground to about 3 metres high and would seem simple aviculture subjects. This has not been found to be so, however, for they are hard to establish and restrict themselves to an inadequate fruit-only diet. It must be emphasized, though, that they have never been imported in more than the odd ones and twos so the collective avicultural experience is very limited.

Although gregarious by nature, they separate at breeding times, males finding a small territory and selecting in it a display area. In some species this will be a little piece of the ground from which the males clear everything and then do their display on the bare earth. The red-capped manakin, however, carries out his display ritual from a tree branch in a sunny position from which he has removed all leaves. The display is quite intricate and increases in tempo at the sighting of a female. It is generally believed that when mating has taken place the female goes off to make a nest, lay eggs and rear the young alone, while the male continues his song and dance routine hoping to attract and so mate with more females.

Whilst numerically very small, there are probably more **Blue-backed manakins** (*Chiroxiphia pareola*) in aviculture than any other species. Captive breeding has taken place and this one species seems the most suited to aviculture.

Quetzals

Quetzal (*Phatomachrus mocinno*)
Grouping: fruit-biased omnivore

The fabulous quetzal is one of the Central American trogons which, together with the three African trogons and the dozen or so from

South-East Asia, go to make up a family to compete with the birds of paradise. Trogons are just as breathtaking as birds of paradise, just as legendary, just as mysterious and, sadly, just as inaccessible. Very few reach aviculture, but the quetzal is represented in some collections and is reasonably well known compared to other trogons.

Quetzals live at very high altitudes, some 3000 metres above sea level in the cold and wet cloud forests, indicating that the last thing they want in captivity is the type of hothouse accommodation one would instinctively provide. The illustration is of a female (some 25 cms long) who is totally overshadowed by the beauty of the male, for which unfortunately a good coloured photograph is not available, when he is in breeding plumage. The male's head, chest and upper parts are shimmering bronze-green. The feathers on the head are fine and look as though they had been brushed upwards and backwards. They are more bristly on the crown and come slightly forward, merging with the bristles all trogons have at the base of their wide beaks. The wing feathers, which would in most birds be referred to as lesser, median, greater and primary coverts, grow very long and curve forward – this can be seen clearly even on the female illustrated. The under parts below the green chest are brilliant red. The two central pairs of upper tail coverts are shimmering green and grow to about 50 cms long.

Having been worshipped by the Aztecs centuries ago, the quetzal is still revered, to the point that the Guatemalans have named their currency after it and have it as their national bird, just as the United States of America have their famous bald-headed eagle.

It is said, though is hard to imagine, that quetzals pluck fruit while hovering and take winged insects in the same way; but coming as they do from remote and inaccessible highlands, it follows that, like most birds of paradise, they are difficult to study. It also follows that birds from such areas are extremely rare in captivity. My own experience is limited to just one pair which were received as immatures in 1970. The male was never quite right and gave the impression of having lost his will to live. The female was quite all right, however, and she proved very willing to adapt to her changed environment. I eventually sold them, the male by that time having improved but still lacking the alertness of his mate. I do not know what subsequently happened to the male but the female was resold recently, having been in captivity for eight years or more. This would confirm that they have a fairly long life and that, in the unlikely event of any more becoming available, they would be not too hard to establish. Although birds from very high altitudes sometimes suffer from lung disorders when brought to lower levels, they are theoretically easier to establish and acclimatize.

Fruitsuckers

Golden-fronted fruitsucker (*Chloropsis aurifrons*)
Grouping: fruit-biased omnivore

Alternatively known as 'chloropsis' or 'leafbirds' these are justifiably one of the most popular of all softbills. To be precise, *Chloropseidae* embraces the six fruitsuckers and also small yellow and green birds slightly similar to zosterops called ioras. The golden-fronted fruitsucker is one of those birds which have been kept as pets for centuries by people in the East, who appreciate their song and mimicry. They often learn to imitate the songs of other birds and are very happy cage birds. Their willing acceptance of captivity, cheerful natures, song and handsome plumage make them the perfect pet.

Aviculturists are very familiar with this abundant bird, both beginners and the experienced alike appreciating its many qualities. On the debit side, one can only say that fruitsuckers are not the most sociable of birds.

The golden-fronted is not sexable by sight so finding a pair can take time but, if this is achieved, a pair will live together *if introduced to their quarters together* and are likely subjects for breeding. They occasionally interest themselves in baskets but will more often construct their own cup-shaped nest in a suitable tree right at the top of the aviary. The nest is fairly shallow, and breeding fruitsuckers become noisy and panicky at the slightest occurrence. Whether breeding or not, golden-fronteds alone may be wintered out – these being the only fruitsucker strong enough – though unless this is necessary it would be more prudent to provide a little warmth.

All six fruitsuckers have the same habits – they are arboreal, live on fruit, insects and nectar from suitable flowers, usually travel in pairs and will mimic the songs of other birds. Orchards, gardens and forest edges are typical habitats. It is a common bird in India, from which most get into aviculture, but ranges also to most South-East Asian countries.

Also illustrated is one of the more unusual fruitsuckers – the **Bluewinged** (*Chloropsis cochinchinensis*) which is exclusively South-East Asian and far more difficult to establish. At about 14 cms, it is smaller than the former, more slenderly built and not possessing such a robust manner. For all that, it is an exceptionally attractive bird (the illustration not doing it justice) and, more importantly perhaps, sexable at a glance. Females are much paler and the colouration less well defined. Coming from more humid jungle habitats, this is a good bird for large tropical houses.

Fairy bluebirds

Asian fairy bluebird (*Irena puella*)
Grouping: fruit-biased omnivore

Opinions differ among those who classify birds as to whether these lovely softbills should belong with the chloropsis and ioras, or whether they should be placed with the orioles. Be that as it may, fairy bluebirds are excellent avicultural subjects, drawing admiration from all who see them.

The Asian species has a wide distribution through India, Burma, Thailand and in fact most of South-East Asia, where it exists in five subspecies. All are broadly alike, the illustration being of a typical male. Females, though attractive, are nowhere near as striking, since their plumage is dull blue with rather more brilliance on the head, and with black flight feathers. They are thrush-sized birds, quite plump but fast fliers, frequenting forests where they live in small flocks except at breeding times when they separate into pairs. Their repetitive call is pleasant though not very melodious.

I remember clearly the first time a consignment of these lovely birds arrived in England. I was about sixteen at the time and in my first job. Most of my wages were spent at a well-known dealer's establishment of the time, and on one occasion he said that he had just received some fairy bluebirds and Rothschild's mynahs, both of which were virtually unknown in British aviculture then, and live specimens of which I had certainly never seen. It was with great excitement that I peered through some grubby wire netting at a small group of these two rarities, and learned that they were both £50 per pair. Though such sums will not buy many softbills today, at that time £50 represented over twelve weeks' wages and was quite beyond my means.

The source of those few probably dried up, as is regularly the case, for that one-off importation was not to be repeated for many years – probably as long as a decade. Then new territories were opened up and quite quickly fairy bluebirds were freely available and have since become well established in all major bird gardens, zoos and private collections. They have proved wonderfully easy to maintain, are hardy enough to winter out provided they are not subjected to frost since their tiny feet are delicate, and will breed. Pairs will accept a shallow cup-shaped nesting basket, lining it with fine grasses and moss, or will build their own rather insecure-looking nest in a dense bush. They prefer height, however, and appear to limit themselves to just two eggs per nest, which are small, olive-grey in colour, with brown speckling especially at the wide end.

Fairy bluebirds are generally docile towards other birds though, not surprisingly, the males become a little quarrelsome at breeding times. There is nothing fairy-like about these birds, with the exception of their feet which, for the size of the bird, are remarkably small, and it is presumably this feature which accounts for their common name.

The other species is the **Black-mantled fairy bluebird** (*Irena cyanogaster*) which is restricted to the Philippines, where four subspecies live on specific islands. Little data exists on them and, as far as I know, no avicultural knowledge. If they were to become available at all, it is reasonable to assume the standard treatment given to *I. puella* would be suitable. Their habits are the same but the black-mantled is greatly different in appearance – males being mauvy-blue from the crown to neck, back and lesser and median wing coverts. The rest of the body is black, the underparts having a purplish sheen. They have the same bright red eye as the familiar *I. puella*, and females are again much duller.

American orioles

Troupial (*Icterus icterus*)
Grouping: insect-biased omnivore

This is perhaps the prettiest of the thirty-odd slim birds with characteristic long, pointed beaks, which inhabit the tropical Central and South Americas, living invariably in large family groups. They are noisy, inquisitive, extremely active, good fliers and famous for their long penduline nests, which hang from trees. The American orioles are not related to the Old World orioles, and generally are not a colourful group – including as they do the plain black giant cowbirds (*Scaphidura oryzivora*) vast numbers of which seem to be everywhere in Central and South America.

The troupial is, however, very striking and at some 22 cms is not easily overlooked, added to which he is very vocal. He makes a good aviary bird being handsome, robust and full of character. He is also capable of winning in the softbill classes at exhibitions but can be a menace in mixed collections, especially where other birds are trying to nest, and has been occasionally guilty of egg stealing. Due to the closure of Colombia as a bird-exporting country, the species is not now so plentiful in European aviculture as it has always been in the past. Nevertheless, quite a few still exist in zoological collections, from whose visitors they attract much admiration.

Hummingbirds

Brown violet-ear (*Colibri delphinae*)
Grouping: nectivore (see Chapter 6 for specific diet)

Fascinating facts surround this exclusively New World family like an aura – their minute size, unbelievable wing beat rate which can reach 200 per second in some species when the males do their courting display, fantastic ornamentation and the jewel-like iridescent plumage of most and much more. Their sheer beauty caused the near-destruction of many species during the last century when literally millions were mindlessly slaughtered so that their spectacular skins could decorate fashionable ladies' hats and clothing. Their skins were also used in the creation of buttons, brooches and similar unimportant fashion products. Ornithologists of the time happily hunted through the consignment of assorted hummingbird skins as they arrived, excitedly catloguing new species. The story is identical to the exploitation of the birds of paradise. Some museum exhibits of hummingbird displays made during the nineteenth century remain today and include examples which have not been seen in a living state, reinforcing the theory that the 'Bogata trade skins', as they were known, caused the extinction of certain species.

Although the world's forests have been explored, and the present-day custodians of them are busily cutting them down, there are still wild places, mainly in the Amazonian region, where exciting discoveries could yet be made. Hummingbirds not seen for years could still exist in localized habitats, and others never seen by Europeans could at any time be discovered. Discounting the latter hypothesis, it is difficult to be precise about the number of hummingbird species in existence. In any event it is over 300 and within this number are a bewildering array of shapes and sizes.

Not all hummingbirds are small. The predictably named giant hummingbird is over 20 cms long. It lives high in the Andes mountains, is not colourful and because of its weight has a slow wingbeat. At the other end of the scale, most general-knowledge enthusiasts know that the smallest bird in the word is the bee hummingbird, several forms of which live in Cuba and the Isle of Pines.

Not all hummingbirds are clad in the typical iridescent plumage, or have flowing tails or facial ornamentation (females of most species being less colourful anyway), and most certainly not all humming-birds are suited to captivity.

During the 1960s and first half of the 1970s a good variety of species came into aviculture and their maintenance had to be learned largely by trial and error combined with known avicultural principles. The formulation of well-balanced nectar foods was perhaps the main success during this period of experimentation, but to date many groups of hummingbirds have proved virtually impossible to estab-lish. It is now possible to define which are likely to die if taken into captivity and which should thrive. There are quite a large number in the latter category and of these the violet-ears are undoubtedly the most ready to adapt to captive conditions and all that establishment implies.

Our subject, the brown violet-ear, is some 10 cms long; males being greyish brown, paler below than above, with rufous edging to the feathers on the back. He has an off-white moustache and an iridescent patch of greeny violet on the throat. His name comes from the glistening violet patch each side of the head, taking in the ear coverts. Females are the same but with less distinct moustache streaks. The brown violet-ear has an extensive range, being, like so many others, more numerous in Colombia, and also occurring on Trinidad.

In a large and heavily planted enclosure such as a tropical house, several may be kept together but where less space is available, only a pair or a single male will be safe. All hummingbirds are aggressive towards each other and are best housed in small heated aviaries, one pair to each.

The other violet-ears thoroughly recommended are the green (*Colibri thalassinus*) and the larger and more heavily built sparkling (*Colibri coruscans*). They are all strong, robust creatures, not needing excessive heat.

Sunbirds

Purple-rumped sunbird (*Nectarinia zeylonicus*)
Grouping: nectivore (see Chapter 6 for specific diet)

With all the fabulous sunbirds to choose from, I have selected our subject on much the same basis as the hummingbird – this particular sunbird is easier than most to maintain in captivity, it is obtainable whereas many are not, it is attractive and not too expensive.

With their long, downward-curved beaks adapted to drinking nectar, small size and shimmering plumage, sunbirds are the Old World counterparts of hummingbirds, although they are not related. Many are African, with perhaps Kenya being where more species are concentrated then elsewhere. Others are from South-East Asia and the purple-rumped is one of these. He is only 9 cms long, the male being beautifully marked with iridescent green crown and shoulder patch. All upper parts are iridescent purple below the crown, and this also extends to the face, throat and upper breast. All remaining underparts are bright yellow, tail and primaries black, with purplish gloss. The female is very dull in comparison (as are most other female sunbirds) being pale yellow below and greyish brown above, with whitish chin.

Generally inoffensive with other birds, even with its own kind outside breeding times, this sunbird is a good subject for any collection. The call is very quiet compared to near relatives. In aviaries during summer, it will clamber about the shrubs in tit-style searching out tiny insects and may even build one of its purselike nests suspended from a twig within a tall bush. Handfuls of very fine grass, cobwebs, hair and small downy feathers strewn around will encourage a pair to build. Two greenish white eggs, with brownish splotches especially at the wide end, form the usual clutch. Enormous quantities of minute insect life are needed in the event of eggs hatching and the controlled liberty method is about the only way that breeding success could be achieved with these or any other sunbirds.

Fruit pigeons

Thick-billed fruit pigeons (*Treron curvirostra*)
Grouping: frugivore

The fruit pigeons are a well-defined group within the large family of pigeons, occurring in Africa but with most species in Southern Asia and Malaya. Most are very colourful, gregarious, strictly arboreal and get their name from the fact that, unlike other pigeons, they live on fruit instead of grain.

Although popular zoological exhibits, they have never caused much excitement among individual aviculturists. This lack of interest is difficult to understand since, with the exception of the very big imperial fruit pigeons (*Duculinae species*) they are very handsome. Green is the dominant colour and this is in sharp contrast to the oranges, pinks and yellows many species have on the breasts. In almost all, sexing is obvious, they will not molest even the tiniest aviary companion and have simple requirements. They should always be housed in aviaries since none of the family are noted for action and are liable to become too fat if caged for long. I suppose it is this lack of activity which detracts from their charm, since most aviculturists seem instinctively to favour active, inquisitive species.

The thick-billed is found in much of South-East Asia in suitably forested areas. It does not migrate, but is known to cover considerable distances in search of fruiting trees and bushes. For this reason its numbers vary from nil to hundreds in typical localities according to the availability of food. Its feathers remain fresh because they are in regular contact with damp leaves high up in the tree tops, though they do not bathe as such. This would mean that in captivity plumage spraying may be necessary unless housed in a planted aviary. It has a surprisingly large gape. That delicate beak can open enough to swallow a large grape whole! A male is illustrated. Females lack the wine-coloured wings.

Of the other species, I have always found these two to be just as easy to maintain as the thick-billed and are approximately the same length of some 25 cms, orange-breasted (*Treron bicincta*) and pink-necked (*T. vernans*).

Parrotbills

Vinous-throated parrotbill (*Paradoxornis webbiana*)
Grouping: insect-biased omnivore

Parrotbills (*Paradoxornithinae*) are a little-known subfamily within the large and complicated babbler family. They inhabit Himalayan countries – Sikkim and Bhutan and parts of China – where they live in small flocks around cultivated areas but more particularly in bamboo forests. They get their name from their short but very powerful beaks, the upper mandible being curved in the fashion of a parrot's, and they move around in the same acrobatic style as tits.

Although there are approximately ten species, I have only kept two and as far as I know no others have been studied in aviculture. Our subject – the vinous-throated – is a completely charming little bird measuring only 9 to 10 cms much of which is accounted for by the tail. It has uncanny similarities to our English long-tailed tit (*Aegithalos cuadatus*) both in habits and appearance if viewed face-on. Sexes are alike and, as would be expected from its range, it is not delicate. Its song is rather feeble, but it is continually active and in my experience very adaptable to captive conditions.

The other species of which we have experience is the **Grey-headed parrotbill** (*P. gularis*) which is almost twice as big and is destructive to growing vegetation, so not so suitable for planted aviaries, although it should have access to bushes in order to maintain long-term health. Its appearance is more striking for, apart from the larger size, it is white below, rufous on wings, back and tail; and has a soft grey face and crown. A thin black line separates the crown from the face, running through the forehead but not quite meeting at the nape. It also has a small black throat patch, and the beak is yellow. Sexes are completely alike. Following the normal acclimatization, this would be able to live outdoors in the winter though it has decidedly aggressive tendencies where any weaker companions are concerned.

Pittas

Giant pitta (*Pitta caerulea*)
Grouping: insectivore

Alternatively known as jewel thrushes, the pittas form a distinctive family comprising some twenty species which mostly live in South-East Asia, although three are Australian and two endemic to Africa. They are all terrestrial, roaming the undergrowth in heavily forested regions, picking up leaves and small stones for the insects that so often lurk underneath. Although they become tame in confinement, pittas are by nature very shy and rarely seen in their natural habitats. They are all beautifully marked – some exceedingly so – though in the gloom of their forest homes, such gaudy colours seem wasted. Most are around 15 cms in length but the giant is nearer 25.

The giant pitta used to be more easily obtained than now, though has never been common in aviculture. It is more striking than the illustration suggests, for the brilliant blue covers the whole back as well as the wings. Pairs are not difficult to tell apart and this species is most excellent as a ground-exhibit in any greenhouse type of aviary or of course the more elaborate zoological tropical houses. They soon lose their shyness and will even follow people about; they will certainly add much interest to the lower levels. They can fly – indeed all pittas can – but apart from when roosting, they are quite happy hopping about the floor. Slightly damp peat is necessary for the floor covering unless it has ground-covering plants or grass, since the feet of pittas are notoriously prone to sores and bumblefoot.

Of the many other pittas which have done well in aviculture, none are more beautiful than the **Gurney's pitta** (*Pitta gurneyi*) which is very localized in mountainous Thailand. It was named by one Mr Hume who is believed to have discovered it in the 1800s, giving one to the famous ornithologist and bird artist John Gould, and writing to him that he was naming the pitta after his friend, another orni-thologist of the day, J. H. Gurney. The male Gurney's is indeed unique in its colouration. It is a medium-sized pitta, the male being a brilliant study in yellow and black, with brilliant cobalt crown and tail. The wings are thrush-brown although cannot be seen in the illustration. Females of the species are various shades of brown, with black barring across the underparts. I shall always kick myself because while trying to do two things at once, I let the male of the last pair I had escape. I watched helplessly as he sailed away over the houses and out of sight and now, some five years later, I wonder if we will ever see this fabulous bird in aviculture again.

Sun-bitterns

Sun-bittern (*Eurypyga helias*)
Grouping: insectivore

These are exceedingly graceful waders, well suited to life in a large greenhouse-type aviary which has a pool and plenty of vegetation. The warm, humid atmospheres of such structures correspond well to the sun-bittern's natural habitat. They are found in many South American countries but are more numerous in Brazil, Guyana and the southern part of Mexico, where they frequent the banks of jungle streams and pools. They are secretive birds, well camouflaged in such habitats and catch a certain amount of frogs and small fish in addition to their main diet of insects. They are sexable and measure around 40 cms in total length.

They should only be housed in the way mentioned above, although they will live in outdoor aviaries during the summer if preferred, providing these too are well planted and have a pool. If the pool is concrete, their feet will benefit by covering the edges with turves and keeping an adjoining area waterlogged. Hard floors must be avoided, the most suitable coverings being damp peat, damp leaf-mould or grass. Sun-bitterns enjoy poking around in damp leaf-mould for insects. They need warmth during the cold months. Whilst ignoring most other birds, they will not tolerate pittas – no doubt because they have similar habits – and can be dangerous towards very small birds.

There are no other birds in the family, but rails would be fairly close to them. Their method of catching fish is identical to that of herons but sun-bitterns are not related to them – obvious differences being their tails, short legs and lack of the heron's upright stance.

Waxwings

Cedar waxwing (*Bombycilla cedrorum*)
Grouping: frugivore

Sexually alike, waxwings are a distinctive genus (*Bombycilla*) comprising three beautiful softbills, only one of which is regularly seen in aviculture. That is the cedar waxwing which breeds in the United States and migrates to the Central American countries for winter. They are gregarious, greedy feeders, have very smooth plumage – almost like velvet – and get their name from the red waxy substance on the tips of the wing secondaries. Measuring some 15 cms, the cedar is a popular softbill for it is docile, has a pleasant disposition and is hardy. Whilst they take insects at breeding times, they are loath to eat anything but an exclusively fruit diet at other times. In small areas, they have similar sluggish habits to fruit pigeons, and often get too fat as a result, but in outside aviaries are as active as most birds and should certainly be housed in this way.

The slightly larger and more heavily built **European** or Bohemian **waxwing** (*B. garrulus*) is another North American, which very occasionally comes as a winter visitor to England. For this reason it has been included on the British Bird list, thus excluding it from British aviculture effectively. Odd specimens are seen at the bigger shows very rarely, being exhibited in the British softbill classes though they could not be sold unless wearing the approved size of closed ring, indicating that they were bred in captivity.

The third waxwing lives in Japan, has a red tip to the tail instead of the more usual yellow, and does not have any wax on the wing feathers. It is unknown in aviculture as far as I am aware though is used to cool temperatures and would logically thrive on the same treatment given to the cedar.

White eyes

Indian white eye (*Zosterops palpabrosa*)
Grouping: nectivore

Although we only see about four species in aviculture, there are over eighty white eyes worldwide, occurring in Asia, Africa and Australia, as well as on numerous islands. The Australian white eye, for example, which does very considerable damage to grape crops, is now widespread in New Zealand too. White Eyes are a highly successful family and their almost global spread is somewhat surprising since they are not powerful fliers so one wonders how they reach so many islands where long distances are involved. Presumably some are introduced by man.

The African white eyes are mainly yellowish and the Asian ones more green, with grey underparts, and within that broad distinction the various species do not differ greatly. They are all small, active birds some 9 to 12 cms in length sharing the common feature of a white eye ring (except in the Lesser Sunda Islands species). In aviculture their common name derives from this, but they are also known equally well as zosterops.

Z. palpabrosa is perhaps the only nectivore suitable for a beginner, since it is far more adaptable and will thrive without the dietary refinements so necessary with most others. Indeed, it will live in a seemingly fit state without any nectar at all, though there is no point in deliberately refusing to supply such a simply made item. When established it will live outdoors during all the year excepting the very coldest months, and adds a good deal of charm to any mixed aviary. When the breeding season approaches, males will sing very attractively, whilst usually restricting themselves to call-notes only at other times. Sexes are alike and it is really only by the song that males can be determined. This is, however, a very cheap softbill and also gregarious, so it is both practical and desirable to purchase several. From these at least one pair is bound to emerge and in a planted aviary, breeding is quite possible. Nests are invariably fixed between two twigs, presumably for stability, and the eggs – pale turquoise in colour and devoid of markings – are narrow. Many years ago I had a pair of white eyes breeding under the controlled liberty method and one day when approaching the aviary saw several flying about inside the aviary. I was puzzled for the young had only been in the nest a week! When I got to the aviary I could see that they had no eye rings! It took some while to realize that what I thought was some sort of miracle was in fact that the white eyes had attracted some chiffchaffs (*Phylloscopus collybita*) into their aviary. Subsequently I discovered that this happens a lot in suitable weather and the sight of a white eye catching gnats on a warm summer evening, along with the surprisingly similar chiffchaffs, is most fascinating.

Glossy starlings

Royal starling (*Cosmopsarus regius*)
Grouping: insect-biased omnivore

Glossy starlings comprise some sixteen species of brilliantly coloured, jaunty and alert African softbills. They tend to be more concentrated to the east of that continent, where typically they inhabit fairly open countryside, often in very dry localities and so are used to a good deal of sunshine. This would suggest difficulties in acclimatization but with the exception of the royal – our initial subject – this is not so.

Apart from its startling beauty, the royal has another distinction within its family – its slender build. The others are plumpish and rather heavy of appearance. The royal feeds on termites to an appreciable extent in the wild and is also able to catch many flying insects. It is reluctant to stray from an exclusively insect diet, unlike its commoner relatives which also take fruit, and is far more susceptible to climatic changes in captivity than others.

The relative difficulties of establishment and acclimatization are compounded by it being rarely exported. Selective export restrictions exist in part of its territory while political instability in others prevents the development of any bird activities, even though it is not rare. In aviculture however it is certainly rare, with examples being limited to just a few zoos and bird gardens with perhaps a dozen held privately. The illustration shows its beauty very well and while all glossy starlings have shimmering plumage, it is the presence of the contrasting yellow which makes the royal so special.

Almost always available are some of the common glossy starlings such as **Purple glossy starling** (*Lamprotornis purpureus*) and **Long-tailed glossy starling** (*L. mevesi*) all of which are very hardy once acclimatized and need no refined management. They tend to be noisy, especially when something happens to excite or frighten them, but are trouble-free subjects and well recommended to beginners. They should be housed with their own kind or equal-sized birds since they develop aggression and will often hound weaker birds. The common glossy starlings are not expensive. They are robust, intelligent and easy to keep having equally impressive qualities as exhibition birds.

Mynahs

Golden-crested mynah (*Mino coronatus*)
Grouping: insect-biased omnivore

Forming another branch of the starling family, mynahs are among the most popular of all avicultural subjects, and have always been so. It is not hard to understand why – they are extremely adaptable and accept captivity well, they are excellent mimics, they are intelligent and alert, completely hardy and the easiest of softbills to manage.

The golden-crested is not one of the most common and will not be known to everybody, but it has a pleasing appearance as can be seen from the illustration. Its glossy black and yellow plumage is common to both sexes, but immatures do not have the yellow at first. It is some 17 cms long and inhabits the forested areas of Indo-China mainly at low levels, but it is recorded up to 1000 metres. Though shy in the wild, it quickly becomes bold in captivity.

Many relatives are widely kept and require little more than the basics of softbill husbandry to remain in perfect health and condition for their long lives.

The distinctive **Rothschild's mynah** (*Leucopsar rothschildi*) represents one of aviculture's success stories. For a long time it has been regarded as an endangered species since development on its restricted island home of Bali in Indonesia has taken much of its natural habitat. Concentrated efforts to breed it in captivity proved remarkably successful, to the extent that captive-bred stock is now commonplace in zoos and bird gardens, together with some of the major private collections. The captive-bred birds have themselves bred on maturing and the future of the species is now assured in aviculture, if not in the wild. It must be admitted, in giving a balanced account of this avicultural success, that mynahs as a group are relatively free breeders and do not require anything hard to provide. Such success would have been far less likely in most other softbill families. Although aviculture is not to blame for birds becoming endangered, it often happens that when they do, captive breeding programmes become the main hope in preventing extinction.

The Rothschild's mynah is completely hardy, although since most are now captive-bred this would be taken for granted, and will associate safely with related birds or other softbills of similar size. It is an excitable bird, but not over-noisy, inquisitive and, because of its colour, provides a welcome contrast when seen against the more usual deep, glossy colours of this family. To emphasize the achievements of aviculture with this species as well as to illustrate its handsome appearance, it is appropriate that the Rothschild's mynah should appear on the front cover.

Tangara tanagers

Paradise tanager (*Tangara chilensis*)
Spangled tanager (*Tangara nigroviridis*)
Golden-eared tanager (*Tangara chrysotis*)
Flame-faced tanager (*Tangara parzudakii*)
Grouping: fruit-biased omnivores

This being one of the best-loved families of all softbills, four have been selected as typical representatives of this important group, instead of the usual single subject. In addition, the range is so large that to choose one species alone does not do this popular family justice. Tanagers from the *Tangara* genus comprise the most well known of the overall family which totals well over 200 species, of which some forty-eight are in fact *Tangaras*. Brazil, Colombia and Ecuador are where most are found, where they frequent forests and search for fruit and insects in small groups. *Tangaras* are sexually alike and average some 10 cms in length. They have little song but, as every aviculturist knows, this is handsomely made up for by their beautiful plumage.

In captivity *Tangara* tanagers are, with very few exceptions, easy subjects to maintain, and if moderate warmth is provided for the cold months, they will be able to stay outdoors continuously *when properly acclimatized*. They will live with other softbills of similar size, for *Tangaras* themselves are docile. Certain species have naturally, or soon develop in aviculture, specific dietary likes and dislikes. In extreme cases, this selectivity can result in malnutrition since too narrow a diet (not balanced) cannot provide the various vitamins necessary to maintain health. The fruit must therefore be chopped in small dices and mixed thoroughly, together with insectile mixture and the other items described in the feeding chapter. In this form, fussy birds find it harder to select just the fruit they like best, and the taste of all the fruits is partly masked by the other ingredients. If, however, large slices of fruit are laid out for them, it virtually invites the birds to select only their favourite type. Further, it is best to calculate the daily food intake fairly accurately, and provide marginally more than they will consume. Invariably all the items then become eaten, whereas they will always pick out their favourites and take nothing else, if separated sliced fruit is given in abundance.

As exhibition softbills, our four subjects are, as with other related species, almost certain to do well. They must be steady of course and not shown before they moult. Though sexing is a hit and miss affair, most of this genus will attempt breeding if a pair can be selected. Small open-cup nest baskets are often chosen, but, as always, plenty of nesting materials and some dense bushes growing in the aviary will encourage them to build their own nest, which is much the best way. In aviaries, of course, the height is usually limited to two metres and most *Tangaras* will build at about that height though in the wild they occasionally nest ten times higher. Both sexes co-operate in nest construction and, unless badly frightened, prove good parents. Those species which have bred (or attempted breeding) for me in the past have always had two eggs – this may be coincidence but suggests that two is the standard *Tangara* clutch. Some species are extremely rare and only known from single museum skins dating back almost a century. Others are quite plentiful and probably a dozen are kept in aviculture continuously, including our four subjects.

The paradise tanager is well named, for its colours are magnificent. Each colour is solid and sharply separated from the next, with no merging of shades. Though the picture is clear it is unable to show the vivid red back which, in flight, becomes more obvious. It ranges from Colombia, Ecuador and Northern Peru across into the Northern part of Brazil where it is a shy forest dweller. This shyness is its only disadvantage in captivity, for the paradise takes longer than most to settle down. It has the infuriating habit of hiding in corners on the ground which usually soils the tail, but with patience this lovely bird can be steadied and, exceptionally, hand tamed.

Though not so striking, the spangled tanager is most attractive, with its many spots being almost luminous. It has a more restricted range and is more insectivorous than the former but is every bit as desirable. Water provided for this species should not be more than about 2 cms deep, for it has similar bathing pecularities to the verditer flycatcher and will easily become chilled.

The golden-eared is another *Tangara* whose plumage shines and can be called luminous in parts. When seen in a planted aviary, it provides a really exotic sight as it flits in and out of vegetation, usually accompanied by a very plain call. It is a forest dweller but tames far quicker than most relatives and, although less numerous than in recent years, it is recommended as an exhibition bird.

There are two races of flame-faced, the difference only being in the amount of red on the face. It is a couple of centimetres bigger than the other *Tangaras* mentioned and represents about the maximum size of any in the genus. This does not make it any hardier but in planted communal aviaries, it does make the species stand out more. As can be seen from the illustration, most of the brilliant colour is concentrated on the head though its plumage throughout is pleasing.

All species of *Tangara* will live peacefully with their own or related species for they are sociable, as well as with other kinds of softbill of similar disposition. In general they are robust and completely suited to cage or aviary life.

Chlorochrysa tanagers

Orange-eared tanager (*Chlorochrysa calliparaea*)
Grouping: insect-biased omnivore

Tanagers from this genus are nowhere near as plentiful in aviculture as the *Tangaras* and have proved more demanding and not so hardy.

They come from forested areas of tropical South America and although relatively little is known of their natural habits, it seems likely that they are strongly insectivorous. Indeed their beaks give this impression, and it has been my experience that they do not thrive well in aviculture unless given significantly more livefood than other tanagers; hence the different dietary grouping.

The captivating little orange-eared is only some 8 to 9 cms long and looks very much the creature of dense forest it is, in shimmering emerald, with black markings and the areas of orange to the face and crown. It is the *vertical* crown stripe which is the most distinctive feature.

There is no logical reason why it should be more delicate than the *Tangara* tanagers but it is – and should only be kept outdoors during the warmest months of the year. It will enjoy being outside at such times and benefit by catching a few insects not provided in a captive diet. A well-planted aviary will naturally suit it best but being docile in the extreme, as well as fairly rare, all companions should be avoided unless significantly smaller.

Large tanagers

Magpie tanager (*Cissopis leveriana*)
Grouping: fruit-biased omnivore

Not all tanagers are small. Within the vast family are several genera of very large ones which have the advantage of being completely hardy and in many cases sexable. In this connection it is interesting that the only four tanagers (*Piranga species*) which migrate into the United States for the summers are all basically red of one shade or another in males and olive yellow in females. Until a few years ago, aviculture was regularly blessed with various mountain tanagers (*Compsocoma species*) which, though not easy to sex, were very attractive and, coming as they do from high altitudes in the Andes, were no problem to acclimatize.

A glance at the illustration will verify that no other name could possibly be given to the 22 cm magpie tanager which, like all other large species, is absolutely perfect for a large outdoor aviary, but not to be trusted with smaller or weaker companions. He has a massive distribution in South America, including cool areas, and has been recorded in Argentina, Bolivia, Paraguay, as well as the normal tanager strongholds. In spite of this it is not seen in aviculture very often which is regrettable as no tanager is more intelligent or easy to manage.